Physical Characteristics of Basset Fauve de Bretagne

(from the Fédération Cynologique Internation

C000230773

Back: Short for a Basset and broad.

Loin: Broad and muscular.

Tail: Carried slightly sickle-fashion, of medium length, large at the base, often bristly and well-tapered at the end. In action, the tail is carried above the top line and makes regular movements from side to side.

Height: Males and females: 32 cm minimum (12.6 in), 38 cm maximum (15.5 in) with a tolerance of 2 cm (0.8 in) for exceptional specimens.

Abdomen: The underline rises only slightly towards the rear.

Hindquarters: Well muscled. The limbs are well poised. Seen from behind, the rear limbs are parallel, neither close nor wide.

Feet: Compact with the toes tight together, arched and with solid nails. The pads are hard.

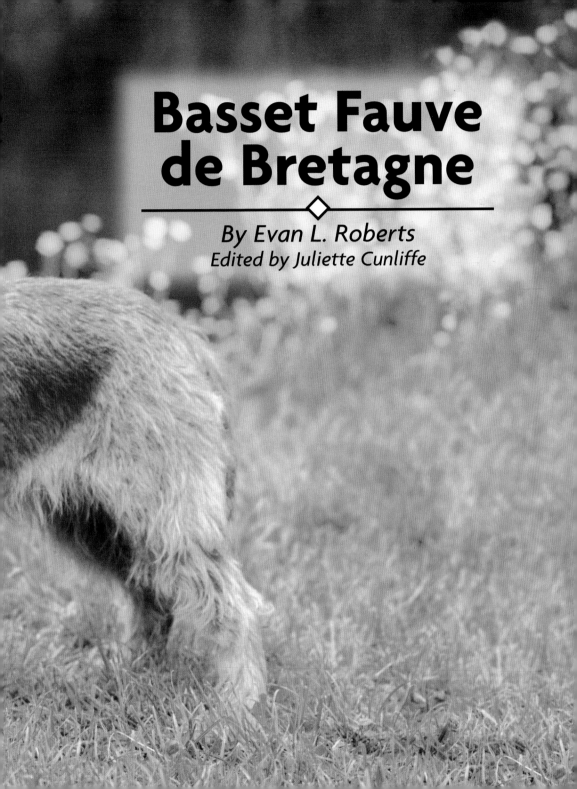

Basset Fauve de Bretagne

By Evan L. Roberts
Edited by Juliette Cunliffe

Contents

9   History of the Basset Fauve de Bretagne

A rough-coated hound from France's Brittany region, the Basset Fauve was developed in response to a need for a short-legged hunting dog. Meet related French hunting breeds and trace the Basset Fauve's beginnings and his rescue from near-extinction, as well as French fanciers' efforts to keep him first and foremost a hunter.

18   Characteristics of the Basset Fauve de Bretagne

Charming, friendly and personality-packed, the Basset Fauve is a small hound with much to offer as a hunting partner or just a companion. Learn all about the breed, in temperament, abilities, physical traits and health concerns, to determine if you are the right person to welcome a Basset Fauve into your heart and home.

29   Breed Standard for the Basset Fauve

Learn the requirements of a well-bred Basset Fauve de Bretagne by studying the description of the breed set forth in the Fédération Cynologique Internationale standard. Both show dogs and pets must possess key characteristics as outlined in the breed standard.

36   Your Puppy Basset Fauve de Bretagne

Find out about how to locate a well-bred Basset Fauve de Bretagne puppy. Discover which questions to ask the breeder and what to expect when visiting the litter. Prepare for your puppy shopping spree. Also discussed are home safety, the first trip to the vet, socialization and solving basic puppy problems.

60   Everyday Care of Your Basset Fauve

Cover the specifics of taking care of your Basset Fauve de Bretagne every day: feeding for the puppy, adult and senior dog; grooming, including coat care, ears, eyes, nails and bathing; and exercise needs for your dog. Also discussed are the essentials of dog identification and traveling with your dog.

Training Your Basset Fauve de Bretagne   82

Begin with the basics of training the puppy and adult dog. Learn the principles of house-training the Basset Fauve de Bretagne, including the use of crates and basic scent instincts. Enter Puppy Kindergarten and introduce the pup to his collar and leash and progress to the basic commands.

Healthcare of Your Basset Fauve de Bretagne   107

By Lowell Ackerman DVM, DACVD
Become your dog's healthcare advocate and a well-educated canine keeper. Select a skilled and able veterinarian. Discuss pet insurance, vaccinations and infectious diseases, the neuter/spay decision and a sensible, effective plan for parasite control, including fleas, ticks and worms.

Your Aging Basset Fauve de Bretagne   138

Know when to consider your Basset Fauve de Bretagne a senior and what special needs he will have. Learn to recognize the signs of aging in terms of physical and behavioral traits and what your vet can do to optimize your dog's golden years.

Behavior of Your Basset Fauve de Bretagne   144

Analyze the canine mind to understand what makes your Basset Fauve de Bretagne tick. Potential problems addressed include: aggression, separation anxiety, sexual misconduct, chewing, digging, jumping up, barking and food-related issues.

Index 156

KENNEL CLUB BOOKS: **BASSET FAUVE DE BRETAGNE**
ISBN: 1-59378-343-4

Copyright © 2004
Kennel Club Books, LLC, 308 Main Street, Allenhurst, NJ 07711 USA
Cover Design Patented: US 6,435,559 B2 • Printed in South Korea

Photography by Carol Ann Johnson
with additional photographs by:

T.J. Calhoun, Carolina Biological Supply, Juliette Cunliffe, Sue Domun, Isabelle Français, Bill Jonas, Dr. Dennis Kunkel, Tam C. Nguyen, Phototake and Alice van Kempen.

Illustrations by Patricia Peters.

The publisher wishes to thank all of the owners whose dogs are illustrated in this book, including the Borrelli family, Raul Gilles and Irene Judd.

The Basset Fauve de Bretagne is a keen hunting hound that brings a winning combination of intensity and charm to the field and home.

BASSET FAUVE DE BRETAGNE

ORIGIN AND DEVELOPMENT

As the breed's name implies, the Basset Fauve de Bretagne's origins lie on the northwestern coast of France, in Brittany. But this is a very old race, though its popularity appears to have declined in the late 19th century and was not truly rekindled until well into the 20th.

Before looking closely at the breed itself, we should begin by considering the time in France when hunting on horseback prevailed. For this, very large and courageous hounds were used in thinly populated areas. One of the breeds used was the Grand Fauve de Bretagne, whose quarry was primarily wolf and wild boar. In other areas of France, hunting was carried out using hounds such as the Chien D'Artois, Griffon Vendéen and Bleu de Gascoigne. Due to the terrain in which they worked, those hounds hunting in heavily wooded areas tended to be rough-coated, while those that hunted in more open areas generally had smooth coats.

The Breton race of men, and indeed the Breton language and traditions, resulted from a series of emigrations and colonizations from Wales, these having taken place towards the end of the fifth century. The country only acquired the name of Brittany when it was colonized by the Britons or Welsh. The previous population of Romanized Gauls was scattered and displaced by the ravages of pirates and barbarian tribes. It is highly probable that the settlers took with them their hunting dogs and, for several centuries, there was close contact between Brittany and Wales, so there was doubtless an exchange of hounds between them.

From these events one might well conclude that the rough-coated strains of hounds originated in Wales, but we should also bear in mind that the ancient Britons originated in Gaul. This means that the Britons' animals were almost undoubtedly of Gallic origin, and indeed the native hounds of Gaul were actually rough-coated. So we can conclude that the rough hounds

GRIFFON FAUVE
One of the ancestors of the Basset Fauve, the Griffon Fauve de Bretagne, was a larger hound, used to track down predators that preyed on flocks of sheep. The Basset Fauve originally hunted game from rabbits to wild boar, usually in small packs of four.

of Brittany, was a large hound standing 27.5–29.25 inches (70–74 cm) at the withers. It was introduced to the French court in about 1520 by Admiral d'Annebaulde, who had a pack of this breed at that time. In the pack was a hound called "Miraud," who was recorded as having been used extensively at stud in the royal pack. However, as soon as the Breton influence was lost, the hounds of Brittany no longer retained their popularity at court.

It is important to bear in mind that until the French Revolution, only the aristocracy was allowed to keep hounds and to hunt. In general, this was done on horseback, so large hounds were needed. In 1789, aristocratic privileges were abolished, meaning that people other than aristocrats could keep hounds and hunt. However, they did not own horses, so the large hound breeds were useless to them. Thus, out of necessity, shorter-legged hounds, the various Bassets, were developed; these dogs can be described as "the true hounds of Egalité!"

The type of those original Breton hounds is preserved in what used to be known as "Breton Bassets." In the early 1920s, Sir John Buchanan-Jardine saw a pack of these little Bassets being exhibited at a Paris show. He considered them charming little hounds, very level in size, type

were actually taken from Gaul to Wales, and subsequently back across the water to Brittany.

We know that François I (1515-1547) had a pack of Breton hounds with which he hunted regularly. These were Grands Fauves de Bretagne, which are sadly now extinct, but their blood runs on in the veins of the rough-coated Griffon and Basset hounds. The Grand Fauve, or Fawn Hound

and color. Their color was a bright reddish fawn, with a little white on the chest in some cases. Two of the dogs showed white blazes down their faces. He considered them rather smaller than most Bassets, but nonetheless they looked active and hardy and had just the stamp to hunt game out of thick cover in rough country. These dogs also struck him as showing a very definite and distinct breed type of their own, slightly different from that of any other French strain.

Two Breton hound breeds still exist today. The Griffon Fauve is the larger of the two, standing 19–22 inches (48–56 cm), while

PURE-BRED PURPOSE

Given the vast range of the world's 400 or so pure breeds of dog, it's fair to say that domestic dogs are the most versatile animal in the kingdom. From the tiny 1-pound lap dog to the 200-pound guard dog, dogs have adapted to every need and whim of their human masters. Humans have selectively bred dogs to alter physical attributes like size, ability, color, leg length, mass and skull diameter in order to suit our own needs and fancies. Dogs serve humans not only as companions and guardians but also as hunters, exterminators, shepherds, rescuers, messengers, warriors, babysitters and more!

Fawn Hounds of Brittany, a now-extinct breed. The dog on the right is a pure-bred, while the others are Vendéen crosses.

Published in *La Chasse Illustré* (Hunting Illustrated) in 1894 was this picture of Bassets Fauves de Bretagne of the Monti de Rézé pack.

the Basset Fauve is 12.6–15.5 inches (32–38 cm), but under the regulations of the Fédération Cynologique Internationale (FCI) there is a tolerance of a further 2 centimeters for top-quality dogs.

Quite how the Basset Fauve came to have been reduced in size is a matter for debate. It may be that, for breeding purposes, undersized specimens were selected from full-sized litters, but it may be that the smallest and slowest were selected for breeding over many generations. However it came about, there is no doubt that by the 19th century many hound packs in France were made up exclusively of Bassets Fauves.

It has long been thought that by the close of World War II, both of these breeds had become virtually extinct. Just a few dedicated French breeders had the temerity to keep a few dogs during those difficult years, resulting in stock available upon which to base the breed's re-creation. However, Mme. F. Corbeau of France's Club du Fauve de Bretagne does not

EARLY FRENCH HOUND TYPES

In the 16th century, there were basically four types of hound in France: the white, known as "du Roi"; the gray, called "du St Louis"; the fawn, known as "de Bretagne" and also a black hound. It is believed that all the French hounds today stem from these four original types.

Modern-day Griffons Fauves de Bretagne, true hunting hounds that are commonly seen in packs or groups.

believe this to have been so. She claims that the breed continued to be popular with huntsmen in the west of France during the early

FRENCH BREEDS ABROAD
Of the French scenthounds, best known outside its country of origin is the Basset Hound, but the two sizes of Basset Griffon Vendéen (Petit and Grand) have become more widely known in recent years. The Basset Fauve de Bretagne also has a dedicated band of followers. The Basset Bleu de Gascoigne is now making an appearance in other countries, including Britain, where some are incorporated in hunting packs and they are occasionally found in the show ring.

years of the 20th century, which ties in with the fact that there were already some dogs of excellent type in the 1950s. Had the breed virtually died out, one could not have expected such a rapid revival in quality.

Although there are but few proven facts, it now seems possible that it was not until the 1970s that French huntsmen introduced new blood by way of the Basset Griffon Vendéen to improve hunting ability and the red Standard Wirehaired Dachshund to keep color.

The Griffon Fauve, used for hunting large game, is still very rare, and was not seen outside its homeland until reaching Sweden

Illustration of Griffon Fauve de Bretagne Fanfare II, owned by M. H. de Lamandé and originally published in the French magazine *L'Eleveur*.

fairly recently. The Basset Fauve, easily capable of clearing fallen trees, hunts rabbit, hare and wild boar. While by no means a numerically strong breed, it has thrived successfully and is now known in several countries throughout the world.

SIR JOHN BUCHANAN-JARDINE'S COMMENTS ON THE BREED IN 1937

Sadly, little has been written specifically about this wonderful little breed, probably because of its mixed fortunes in recent centuries. However, Sir John Buchanan-Jardine wrote about the breed in 1937, and I feel that the best service I can do the author is to directly quote that which he wrote:

"These charming little hounds of a most distinctive appearance are unfortunately not to be found in any great number in France at present, and those that one sees often show traces of crossing with the Griffon Vendéen. However, there are still a few regular breeders of them who carry on the strain in its purity…

"These Bassets give one the impression of greater activity and sharpness than any other type, partly perhaps from being rather shorter coupled and partly from their very alert expression of countenance. I believe them to be very useful hounds in the field, particularly in rough, steep or rocky country where other Bassets would be at a disadvantage, and I imagine the reason the breed has not gained more adherents is the fact that they are, like their ancestor the full-sized Breton hound, apt to be very riotous and hard to break; also the fact that in the point of music they hardly come up to other breeds. As the latter particular is one of the outstanding features of Bassets and one of the principal points that their admirers look for, perhaps their comparable lack of popularity may be largely traceable to this. Such as it is, however, the type is a very characteristic one and it seems rather a pity that it is to be met with in so few kennels to-day."

THE BASSET FAUVE'S RE-CREATION

Although Mme. Corbeau's views put a different perspective on things, it is generally believed that following World War II, the few remaining pure Bassets Fauves were crossed with Bassets Griffons Vendéens and red-colored Standard Wirehaired Dachshunds. The result was the re–creation of the smallest French hound, which, though lacking in stature, most certainly lacks nothing in ability or heart. This is a breed that thrives on work and has a reputation of being "excessivement meurtier," which can be loosely translated to include the words "deadly, "murderous" and "blood-thirsty!" The Basset Fauve, like his cousin the Griffon Fauve, has always been noted for his enormous courage and first-rate scenting abilities.

In France, the breed's recovery was relatively swift. Today many Basset Fauve owners use the breed for hunting purposes, as perhaps indicated by the motto of the French breed club's motto, "Chasse d'aborde," meaning "hunting first." However, others are kept purely as companions around the home, and others as show dogs.

THE BREED IN BRITAIN AND BEYOND

By the closing years of the 19th century, many of the Basset breeds had begun to spread beyond France to neighboring countries, and the Basset Fauve was no exception. Indeed it had become fairly common in the Low

WORLD WINNER
At the World Dog Show in Verona, Italy in 1980, it was a Basset Fauve de Bretagne that had the great honor of winning Best in Show. Truly the breed has made rapid strides since its near-extinction by the close of the World War II.

she was whelped in 1977. She produced a litter comprising two dogs and a bitch, and thus began the breed's career in the UK. Two years later, Hercule Ter Elst came to Britain from Belgium and Fatima Pooh Corner from the Netherlands. Jolie Mogway of Pooh Corner was imported next, coming from the Netherlands in 1987. The author is happy to report that he imported these four Bassets Fauves, and their progeny firmly established the breed in Britain. Further imports to Britain followed during the 1990s, not only from the Netherlands and from France but also from Sweden. These importations thereby increased the bloodlines available, something that is so important when dealing with a relatively small gene pool.

In recent years, with the relaxation of quarantine laws for dogs coming into Britain, it has been easier for British breeders to import stock from Europe, which, if done wisely, can only be for the long-term benefit of the breed.

Happily, the breed did not increase in popularity too quickly in Britain, despite the fact that it was certainly noticed by the canine fraternity. Open Show societies sometimes provided classes for the Basset Fauve, and eventually the breed also was separately classified at Championship shows.

In 1991, the Basset Fauve breeders and owners formed a

Countries and in Denmark. It was no surprise that the breed made its way to the British Isles.

Naika Des Vieilles Combes was the first Basset Fauve to arrive in Britain; this was in 1982. She arrived from France, where

Examples of
today's winning
Bassets Fauves:
bitch on the left
and dog on the
right.

breed club to administer and
supervise the affairs of the breed,
with a committee elected to
manage the club's business.
Regular meetings were held in the
form of seminars, thus enabling
more people, including aspiring
judges, to learn more about the
Basset Fauve de Bretagne.

In Britain some Bassets
Fauves are used to hunt in
packs, similar to the way in
which the Beagle is thus
occupied. However, the majority
in the UK are kept as family pets
and as show dogs, although the
breed is still classified as a "Rare
Breed" and thus is not yet
eligible for championship status.
However, dedicated owners will

always find opportunities to
exhibit their beloved breed. At a
recent Crufts show, 50 represen-
tatives of the breed were entered,
definitely proving that the breed
has come a long way from what
many believe to have been near-
extinction.

RISING REGISTRATIONS

In France, numbers of registrations for
the Basset Fauve de Bretagne have
risen considerably in recent decades.
In 2002, there were 1060 new registrations, which remarkably equates to
more than the combined registrations
of Bassets Griffons Vendéens for that
year. In Britain, the annual registration
figures for the breed barely reach 100.

CHARACTERISTICS OF THE

BASSET FAUVE DE BRETAGNE

The Basset Fauve de Bretagne is a great little dog, full of character and with an amiable personality. The breed is a sensible size, which means that it will fit in easily with most households, with food bills that will not be enormous. The Basset Fauve does not require a great deal of coat care, though general grooming is, of course, an important aspect of any dog's management.

You may decide that this is just the breed for you, although you might just have difficulty finding one, as this is a rare breed and completely unknown in some countries. In those countries where there is more than a handful of Bassets Fauves being shown, there is likely to be a national breed club, the secretary of which will undoubtedly be pleased to give you sound advice and point you in the right direction to begin your search. Should you have difficulty locating a breed club, your country's national kennel club or a registry that recognizes the breed should be able to help.

PERSONALITY

Although a quiet, affectionate dog, the Fauve is courageous and strong-willed. As such, determined training is necessary from an early age if you do not wish your dog to get the "upper hand." When hunting, the breed is tenacious and vigorous. Because this is a very nimble breed, a Basset Fauve can be quicker than you think, so always be on the alert when exercising your dog off lead, only doing so in securely enclosed areas.

With his family, the Basset Fauve is highly affectionate and

TRUE TO TYPE
It is likely that in its formative years the Basset Fauve de Bretagne was more terrier-like in general appearance. In the countries where the breed is known, it is becoming increasingly uniform in type, but height still varies somewhat. It is generally believed that the breed's type, size and proportions are most uniform in France, but other countries are striving to equal this.

The Basset Fauve is a short-legged, relatively long-bodied dog with a rough coat and handsome facial furnishings. As a hunting dog, he is right at home in the great outdoors.

responsive. He gets along well with children, although introductions between children and dogs should always be done sensibly and supervised carefully, whatever the breed.

Although a hound with a good nose, and bred to work with a pack, the Fauve usually gets along well with other pets. Once again, early socialization and careful initial introductions are a must.

Breeders of the Basset Fauve are determined to retain the sweet nature of this breed, which is lively, friendly and amenable. This is a wonderful little character that is cheerful, outgoing and lots of fun to be with!

PHYSICAL CHARACTERISTICS

OVERALL BODY STRUCTURE
A fairly small, short-legged, rough-coated hound, the Basset

RAISING PUPPY RIGHT

To help him fit well into his environment, socializing your Basset Fauve from an early age is important. Basic training can begin as early as eight weeks of age, paying special attention to interaction with adults, children and other dogs, although your Fauve is unlikely to show any aggression toward them. It is important that your Fauve knows that you are the boss. Obedience training, especially the recall exercise, should be taught early.

should turn neither in nor out, and when the dog is standing naturally, his legs are just under the body. The forelegs are straight and well boned, but a slight crook is acceptable. The pasterns are strong and the feet should not turn outward. The foot pads should be firm and hard, the nails short.

Constructed in this way, the Basset Fauve can move quickly, striding out well. In France the breed's movement is described simply as "lively."

As previously mentioned, the breed standard asks for a height at the withers of 12.6 – 15.5 in (32-38 cm), plus the FCI's allowance of an additional 2 cm for top-quality dogs.

HEAD

The head is set on a rather short, muscular neck. Overall, the head is of medium length, with a moderately domed skull of fair width. The occipital point, at the back of the skull, should be well defined. The muzzle itself is also of medium length and just slightly arched, with a moderate stop between the eyes. Because this is a working hound, the underjaw should be strong. The nostrils should be wide open and the nose black, or otherwise very dark.

The eyes are slightly oval and must be neither too deep-set nor too prominent. In color they are

Fauve de Bretagne is of a size and structure that will fit in with most households. Although relatively low to the ground, the breed is neither so low as the better-known Basset Hound nor so long in body.

The Fauve's chest is wide and deep, with a prominent sternum. Ribs are well rounded and carried well back. The topline should be level and the loin strong, while the hindquarters are strong and muscular, such a necessary trait for a hound that was bred to work. The stifles are well bent and the hocks well let down, with good angulation. The hind legs

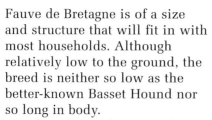

dark or hazel, giving a lively expression. There should be no haw showing in this breed, which does not have the loose skin of the Basset Hound.

The jaws should be strong, and the Fauve has a standard canine bite called a "scissor bite," meaning that the upper teeth closely overlap the lower ones. The teeth should of course be set square to the jaw, with no hint of a wry mouth.

EARS
Because this is a scenthound, the Basset Fauve's ears hang down and extend to the nose when drawn forward, folding inwards and ending in a point. The ear set is level with the eye, and the ears themselves are covered with hair that is darker and softer than that on the body.

TAIL
The tail is high set, thick at the base and tapering to a point. When the dog is moving, the tail

FAMILY DOG
Although the Basset Fauve is likely to announce the arrival of a stranger at your door, this is by no means a guard dog and should never be treated as such. Fauves like to have busy lives and be involved with family life in general. Understandably, the Basset Fauve can become unhappy if left alone for too-long time periods.

The eyes are dark brown, with dark pigmentation of the eye rims, nose and lips, creating a striking contrast against the fawn-colored coat.

The Basset Fauve's head is set on a short, muscular neck and he has "scenthound ears," hanging down and extending to the nose when drawn forward.

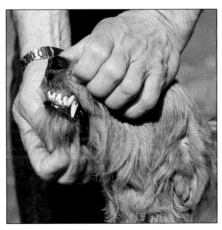

The jaws must be strong with a scissor bite, meaning that the upper teeth closely overlap the lower teeth.

is carried like a sickle. When the tail is lowered, its length reaches slightly below the hock.

COAT AND COLOR

The Basset Fauve de Bretagne has a very harsh, dense, flat coat, which is never long or woolly. The FCI describes the coat in detail, saying that it should be "...dry to the touch, quite short, never woolly nor frizzy" and that the face should not be "tousled."

Colors are fawn, gold-wheaten or red-wheaten. In France the latter two colors are considered the best shades. Although a white spot on the chest is not to be encouraged, this is permissible and can occur occasionally.

CRUCIATE LIGAMENT RUPTURE

The cruciate ligaments that cross each other in the stifle joint are important to maintain stability. Rupture of the cranial cruciate ligament is an injury that is more likely to affect larger breeds of dog, more especially those that are old or overweight.

Slight lameness can be improved with rest, but, in many cases, surgery is necessary. Sometimes the first sign of rupture is sudden, with the dog's being in evident pain; in other cases, the lameness is intermittent, though gradually worsening with time. Many different surgical techniques are employed to stabilize the stifle, but all require careful post-operative care.

Truly a pack hound, the Basset Fauve allows all kinds of dogs in his circle of friends. This Basset Fauve and his Boxer buddy pair up for a little exploring.

Playful, athletic and happy, the Basset Fauve is a fun friend to hang out with!

HEALTH CONSIDERATIONS

When considering if a particular breed is right for you, you must also consider the health concerns specific to that breed. Fortunately, there are currently no known hereditary defects in the Basset Fauve de Bretagne, but all breeds encounter health problems of one sort and another. Some are more prevalent in certain breeds than in others, but to be forewarned is to be forearmed, so the following section may be helpful. It is important that any health problems are dealt with as early as possible, and in the most appropriate manner.

SKIN PROBLEMS AND ALLERGIES

Skin problems and allergies are often difficult to treat success-fully, but unfortunately dogs of any breed can suffer from them. Such problems can often be kept under control with a carefully considered diet. An allergy may be noticed by the appearance of "hot spots" on the skin, despite no sign of external parasites. A low-protein diet often seems to help ameliorate skin troubles.

It is often extremely difficult to ascertain the cause of an allergy. There are many possibilities, ranging from the living room carpet, the shampoo used when

bathing and, quite frequently, certain grasses and molds. In cases of skin allergy, it is a good idea to change shampoo, conditioning rinse and any other coat sprays used, for these are perhaps the easiest items to eliminate before looking further if necessary.

The earlier the symptoms are found, the sooner they can be dealt with, making life much more comfortable for the dog.

Demodectic mange, also known as red mange, is seen in both dogs and cats and is usually due to an immune defect that fails to control the number of mites that are present on the skin of all animals, including humans. A mite population explosion results in bacterial infection. Further, the mites produce substances that compromise the immune system, hence perpetuating the infestation. This type of mange can also be induced by stress, such as when a dog has been shipped abroad or is undergoing hormonal changes.

Balding patches, in which the skin is red and itchy, are typical symptoms. A veterinary skin scrape can diagnose the problem, which fortunately is treatable.

TOOTH AND EAR CARE

Because of the shape of the Basset Fauve's drop ears, they

The Basset Fauve is a plucky little hound, full of enthusiasm and ready for new adventures with the owner he loves.

FOLLOW YOUR NOSE!

Although a Basset Fauve does not need an enormous amount of exercise, some activity is always necessary. Your Fauve will probably be quite happy to accept as much exercise as you give him. When exercising him, always remember that you have a scenthound, which means that he is likely to take off unexpectedly when his nostrils find something interesting! For this reason, especially when exercising near roads or railways, an extended lead is safer than allowing him free run.

should be regularly checked for signs of infection, usually noticed initially by bad odor. Some dogs have a slightly narrow ear canal and, in such cases, ear problems are more likely.

It is also important to pay close attention to the teeth and gums so that they remain as healthy as possible, thereby preventing decay, infection and resultant loss. If infection is evident in the gums, it must be dealt with promptly. A gum

When cleaning the ears, a cotton swab should only be used with the steadiest of hands and the best-trained of dogs. To avoid probing into the ear canal and causing injury, a cotton ball or pad is much safer.

infection may not just stop there. The bacteria can be carried through the bloodstream, the result of which can be diseases of the liver, kidneys, heart and joints. This is all the more reason to realize that efficient dental care is of utmost importance throughout a dog's life.

Feeding dry foods is recommended by many as a means of helping to keep teeth clean and in good condition. Of course, regular careful brushing with a veterinary toothpaste can help enormously. You can use a doggie toothbrush or a fingertip applicator to brush your dog's teeth; also available currently is a special paste that can be applied to the teeth with your finger, helping to remove tartar without the necessity for brushing.

EYE INFECTIONS

Always be sure to stay abreast of the cleanliness and condition of your Basset Fauve's eyes to prevent eye infections' arising. At the first sign of injury, especially if the eye is starting to turn blue in color, urgent veterinary attention is required. Early diagnosis and treatment can often save a dog's sight.

HEART PROBLEMS

Occasionally dogs can suffer from heart problems, particularly as they become more advanced in age. Your vet should always check your dog's heart anytime you visit, whether for a routine examination, vaccinations or anything else.

ARTHRITIS

A frequent cause of arthritis, which can sometimes be found in older dogs, is that the coat has been left wet following exercise in rainy or damp weather. It is therefore wise to dry the dog's coat thoroughly so that it is not allowed to remain damp.

THE OVERWEIGHT DOG

Many dogs have a tendency to gain weight quickly if they are overfed. This also particularly applies to bitches that have been spayed. It is therefore prudent to keep tabs on your Basset Fauve's weight, for a dog carrying excess weight tends to be less healthy than one of the correct weight for his breed. The dog also will be less likely to cope well with anesthetics should an operation ever be necessary.

HEAT EXHAUSTION

Any breed of dog can suffer from heat exhaustion. Frequently, people do not realize how quickly death can result. The first sign of heat exhaustion is heavy panting, and the dog begins to puff or gasp for air. When walking, the dog appears dizzy and tends to weave, subsequently collapsing with eventual unconsciousness.

At the first sign of the dog's being overheated, he should be taken out of the sun and offered water. The body should be doused in cool water, especially the head and neck. If available, ice bags or even a package of frozen vegetables should be placed around the dog's head and neck. Because lowering the dog's temperature is urgent, it should be done right away, even before taking your dog to a vet.

Panting is a dog's way of releasing heat. Heatstroke is dangerous for dogs, so look for signs that your Basset Fauve may need to rest, get a drink of water or spend some time in the shade.

At conformation shows, a dog's quality is measured by how closely he conforms to the official standard, or description, for his breed, thus the name "conformation" shows.

BREED STANDARD FOR THE

BASSET FAUVE DE BRETAGNE

INTRODUCTION TO THE BREED STANDARD

Worldwide, the Basset Fauve de Bretagne is a rare breed, known in a limited number of countries. It is not recognized by the American Kennel Club. In fact, at this time, there are only two recognized breed standards, the French one, which is that adopted by the FCI, and the British standard, approved by The Kennel Club. The two are indeed very similar, the major differences being that the FCI's wording is more detailed and that the FCI standard lists a number of specific faults.

All breed standards are designed effectively to paint a picture in words, though each reader will almost certainly have a slightly different way of interpreting those words. After all, were everyone to interpret a breed's standard in exactly the same way, there would only be one consistent winner within the breed at any given time! A breed standard guides breeders in producing stock that comes as close as possible to the recognized standard. The standard also helps judges to know exactly what they are looking for in the ring. This enables judges to make carefully considered decisions when selecting the most typical Basset Fauve present to head the line of winners.

To fully comprehend the intricacies of a breed, reading words alone is never enough. In addition, it is essential for devotees to give themselves every possible opportunity to come into contact with as many Bassets Fauves as possible. In countries where the breed is actively shown, you should make every effort to watch them being judged in the ring. Breed clubs often host seminars at which the breed is discussed, and there may even be some dogs available for assessment. "Hands on" experience, providing an opportunity to assess the structure of dogs, is always valuable, especially for those who hope ultimately to judge the breed. Taking advantage of every opportunity to observe and learn more about the Basset Fauve enables you to absorb as much as possible about the breed you love.

Whether you are new to the Basset Fauve or very familiar with the breed, it is always worth reading and studying the standard, for it is sometimes all too easy to overlook, or perhaps even forget, certain features. The standard presented here is that of the breed's homeland, France, and is the official standard recognized by the FCI.

THE FCI STANDARD FOR THE BASSET FAUVE DE BRETAGNE

TRANSLATION
John Miller and Raymond Triquet.

ORIGIN
France.

DATE OF PUBLICATION OF THE ORIGINAL VALID STANDARD
March 25, 2003.

UTILIZATION
Scent hound used for hunting rabbit, hare, fox, roe deer and wild boar.

FCI CLASSIFICATION
Group 6, Scent hounds and related breeds. Section 1.3, Small-sized hounds. With working trial.

BRIEF HISTORICAL SUMMARY
This little Basset has the same

Illustration of a Basset Fauve with correct type, balance and soundness.

qualities as the breed from which it is derived: the Griffon Fauve de Bretagne. Very popular in its region of origin in the XIX century, it earned a national reputation in the course of the last 30 years of the XX century. Its exceptional aptitude for hunting has allowed it to win the French Cup hunting trophy on rabbit a number of times and it has become very popular.

Basset Fauve head study depicting correct type, balance and structure.

GENERAL APPEARANCE

The Basset Fauve de Bretagne is a small, stocky hound, lively, rapid for its size. It benefits from enormous energy coupled with excellent hardiness.

BEHAVIOR/TEMPERAMENT

The Bassets Fauves de Bretagne are impassioned hunters but are also excellent companions of man, sociable, affectionate and equable. They adapt themselves easily to all terrains, even the most difficult, and to all quarry. When hunting they reveal themselves to be courageous, wily and obstinate, which makes them very successful.

HEAD

Cranial Region: Skull: Rather long with marked occipital protuberance. Seen from the front, the cranium has the form of a flattened arch and diminishes in width from the rear to the superciliary arches, which are not very prominent. Stop: A little more marked than that of the Griffon Fauve de Bretagne.

Facial Region: Nose: Black or dark brown. Well-open nostrils. Muzzle: Slightly tapering rather than being perfectly rectangular. Lips: Covering well the lower jaw but without excess. Moustaches only slightly furnished. Jaws/Teeth: The jaws and teeth are strong, meeting in a perfect and even scissors bite. The upper incisors cover the lower in close contact. The incisors are set square to the jaws. Absence of first premolars is not penalized. Eyes: Neither bulging nor set too deeply in the orbits, dark brown in color. The conjunctiva is not apparent. The expression is lively. Ears: Finely attached, in line with the eye, just reaching the end of the nose when drawn forward, ending in a point, turned inwards

and covered by finer and shorter hair than on the rest of the body.

NECK
Rather short and well muscled.

BODY
Back: Short for a Basset and broad. Never swaybacked. Loin: Broad and muscular. Chest: Deep and broad. Ribs: Rather rounded. Abdomen: The underline rises only slightly towards the rear.

TAIL
Carried slightly sickle-fashion, of medium length, large at the base, often bristly and well-tapered at the end. In action, the tail is carried above the top line and makes regular movements from side to side.

LIMBS
Forequarters: Overview: The limbs have good bone. Shoulder: Oblique and well set on the thorax. Elbow: In the line with the body. Forearm: Vertical or curving slightly in (which is not to be sought after). Metacarpus (Pastern): Seen in profile, somewhat oblique. Seen from the front, in the axis of the body or slanting slightly out (which is not to be sought after).
Hindquarters: Overview: Well muscled. The limbs are well poised. Seen from behind, the rear limbs are parallel, neither close nor wide. Thigh: Long and well muscled. Hock: Well let down and moderately bent. Metatarsus (rear pastern): Vertical.

FEET
Compact with the toes tight together, arched and with solid nails. The pads are hard.

GAIT/MOVEMENT
Lively.

SKIN
Rather thick, supple. Absence of dewlap.

COAT
Hair: Coat very rough, harsh, rather short, never woolly or curly. The face shouldn't be too bushy.

    Color: Fawn colored, from golden wheaten to red brick in hue. A few black hairs dispersed on the back and ears are tolerated. Occasionally the presence of a small white star on the chest, something not sought after.

HEIGHT
Males and females: 32 cm minimum (12.6 in), 38 cm maximum (15.5 in) with a tolerance of 2 cm (0.8 in) for exceptional specimens.

FAULTS
Any departure from the foregoing points should be considered a fault and the seriousness with which the fault should be regarded should be in exact proportion to its degree.

SEVERE FAULTS
Behavior:
• Timid

Head:
• Wide, flat skull. Superciliary arches too prominent,
• Short or pointed muzzle. Heavy and pendulous upper lips.

This Basset Fauve aptly demonstrates the breed's lively gait.

Eyes:
• Light.

Ears:
• Flat and large

Body:
• Frail in appearance. Top line not level enough. Too tucked up.

Tail:
• Out of line.

Limbs:
• Poor bone. Splayed feet.

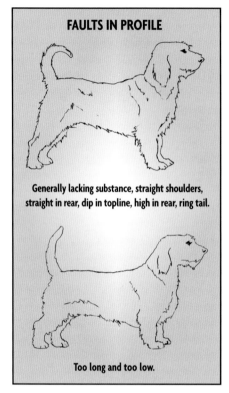

FAULTS IN PROFILE

Generally lacking substance, straight shoulders, straight in rear, dip in topline, high in rear, ring tail.

Too long and too low.

Coat:
• Sparse, smooth, fine, soft.

ELIMINATING FAULTS
Temperament:
• Aggressive or overly shy.

Lack of type:
• Insufficient breed characteristics, which means the animal on the whole doesn't resemble other samples of the breed.

Jaws/Teeth:
• Overshot or undershot.

Eyes:
• Overly light.

Pigmentation:
• Totally or partially unpigmented areas on the nose or the edges of eyelids or lips.

Small dogs are placed on a table for evaluation, to better enable a hands-on examination by the judge.

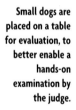

Tail:
• Kinked.

Forequarters:
• Excessive crook.

Dewclaws:
• Presence of dewclaws (this breed is always free from dewclaws).

Coat:
• Long, woolly coat. Any coat

Junior handler with two fine examples of the breed.

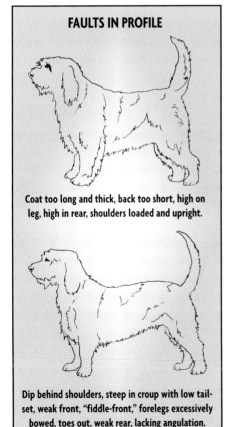

FAULTS IN PROFILE

Coat too long and thick, back too short, high on leg, high in rear, shoulders loaded and upright.

Dip behind shoulders, steep in croup with low tail-set, weak front, "fiddle-front," forelegs excessively bowed, toes out, weak rear, lacking angulation.

other than that defined by the standard.

Height:
• Outside the limits defined by the standard.

Defects:
• Noticeable invalidating defect. Anatomical malformation

Any dog clearly showing physical or behavioral abnormalities shall be disqualified.
N.B.: Male animals should have two apparently normal testicles fully descended into the scrotum.

BASSET FAUVE DE BRETAGNE

PEDIGREE VS. REGISTRATION CERTIFICATE

Too often new owners are confused between these two important documents. Your puppy's pedigree, essentially a family tree, is a written record of a dog's genealogy of three generations or more. The pedigree will show you the names as well as performance titles of all dogs in your pup's background. Your breeder must provide you with a registration application, with his part properly filled out. You must complete the application and send it to the rare-breed registry with the proper fee. Every puppy must come from a litter that has been registered by the breeder, and from a sire and dam that are also registered with a reputable registry.

The seller must provide you with complete records to identify the puppy. The registry may require that the seller provide the buyer with the following: breed; sex, color and markings; date of birth; litter number (when available); names and registration numbers of the parents; breeder's name; and date sold or delivered.

HOW TO SELECT A PUPPY

The Basset Fauve de Bretagne is still not very well known, except by a small band of enthusiasts in a few countries of the world. So before deciding that this really is the breed that will suit your domestic circumstances and lifestyle, you will need to seek out a few owners to give yourself opportunities to meet the breed. You will be extremely fortunate if you have a breeder in your home state; most likely you will have to do some traveling to meet breeders and owners. Your best bet is to make a trip to a dog show at which the breed is being exhibited so you can acquaint yourself with several people in the breed and meet a few dogs. Contacting a breed club is a wonderful way to gain information, but it will likely to be just as difficult to find a Basset Fauve club in your area. The Internet is a great way to contact people in the breed from other countries who can give you advice about your puppy search.

Before beginning your efforts to find a Basset Fauve puppy, it is essential that you are positive that this is absolutely the most suitable breed for you and for your family. You should have carefully examined your family situation and living environment, and taken every aspect of the breed's character and physical makeup into consideration. Remember that the dog you select should remain with you for the duration of his life, which is usually from 12 to 14 years with the Basset Fauve, so making the right decision from the outset is of utmost importance. No dog should be moved from one home to another simply because his owners were thoughtless enough not to have done sufficient research and decision-making before selecting the breed.

Your Basset Fauve should only be purchased from a breeder who has earned a reputation for consistently producing dogs that are mentally and physically sound. In a breed so small numerically, you have the assurance that the breeders are dedicated to preserving this breed, which has only relatively recently been re-established, through rigid ethics in their breeding programs. These same people are very much aware of who else in the breed does or does not ascribe to the breed club's strict code of ethics. In fact, breeders who maintain membership in a breed club, in countries where one exists, monitor their litters carefully in order to avoid

SIGNS OF A HEALTHY PUPPY
Healthy puppies are robust little fellows who are alert and active, sporting shiny coats and supple skin. They should not appear lethargic, bloated or pot-bellied, nor should they have flaky skin, runny or crusted eyes or noses. Their stools should be firm and well formed with no evidence of blood or mucus.

defects of any kind. These are the individuals that you can depend upon to obtain a sound, well-bred and well-socialized representative of the Basset Fauve de Bretagne breed.

The first question a prospective owner should ask a Basset Fauve breeder is, "What do you do with your dogs?" If the person you are talking to breeds Bassets Fauves

MAKE A COMMITMENT
Dogs are most assuredly man's best friend, but they are also a lot of work. When you add a puppy to your family, you also are adding to your daily responsibilities for the next 10 to 15 years. Dogs need more than just food, water and a place to sleep. They also require training (which can be ongoing throughout the lifetime of the dog), activity to keep them physically and mentally fit and hands-on attention every day, plus grooming and health care. Your life as you now know it may well disappear! Are you prepared for such drastic changes?

possibly hunt with their dogs or compete with them in hunting events and are adamant about proper socialization of their dogs.

The first clue that tells you how much the breeder cares about his dogs is the cleanliness of the area in which the dogs are kept. The next is how well socialized the parents of the litter are. Those two conditions met, you can proceed to look at the puppies themselves.

It is always important to remember that, when looking for a puppy, a good breeder will be assessing you as a prospective new owner just as carefully as you are selecting the breeder. The breeder may ask you so many questions that you may feel you are on trial! In a way, you are. Good breeders are very protective of the Basset Fauve's small population. The breeder must consider whether or not you would make a good owner of one of his Basset Fauve pups and, if so, which puppy in the litter would be most suitable for you.

Litter size in the breed is variable, but six pups seems about average. The Basset Fauve puppy you select should be a happy and bouncy extrovert. However, you need not necessarily select the leader of the little pack. The extremely bold and extroverted pup may prove to be a bit more than the inexperienced Basset Fauve owner is equipped to handle. This does not mean you

only to sell, which will be very unlikely in this breed, continue on your search and go somewhere else for your dog! Dedicated Basset Fauve breeders belong to their breed club, compete at shows,

It's an exciting day when the breeder hands over your new puppy to take home with you.

NEW RELEASES

Most breeders release their puppies between seven and ten weeks of age. A breeder who allows puppies to leave the litter at five or six weeks of age may be more concerned with profit than with the puppies' welfare. However, some breeders of show or working breeds may hold one or more top-quality puppies longer, occasionally until three or four months of age, in order to evaluate the puppies' career or show potential and decide which one(s) they will keep for themselves.

should look well fed, but not pot-bellied, as this might indicate worms. His eyes should look bright and clear, without discharge. The nose should be moist, an indication of good health, and it goes without saying that there should certainly be no evidence of loose bowels or of parasites. The healthy Basset Fauve puppy's breath smells sweet. The teeth are clean and white, and there should never be any malformation of the mouth or jaw. The puppy you choose should also have a healthy-looking coat, an important indicator to good health internally. Coughing and diarrhea are danger signals, as are any eruptions on the skin.

The healthy Basset Fauve puppy's front legs should be straight and strong. Even at an early age, soundness in the Basset Fauve puppy should be evident, allowing for puppy awkwardness. Still, movement is true and there should be no hint of lameness or difficulty in movement.

If you are considering a show career for your puppy, you should be aware that the most any breeder can offer is an opinion on the "show potential" of a young puppy. Any predictions that a breeder makes about a puppy's future are based upon the breeder's experience with past litters that have produced winning show dogs. It is obvious that the more successful a breeder has been in producing winning

should select a shy, shrinking-violet puppy, as this is not typical of correct Basset Fauve attitude at all.

The puppy you select should have been well socialized and

Bassets Fauves over the years, the broader his base of comparison will be. Give serious consideration to both what the standard says a show-type Basset Fauve must look like and to the breeder's recommendations.

YOUR BASSET FAUVE SHOPPING LIST

Just as expectant parents prepare a nursery for their baby, so should you ready your home for the arrival of your Basset Fauve pup. If you have the necessary puppy supplies purchased and in place before he comes home, it will ease the puppy's transition from the warmth and familiarity of his mom and littermates to the brand-new environment of his new home and human family. You will be too busy to stock up and prepare your house after your pup comes home, that's for sure. Imagine how a pup must feel upon being transported to a strange new place. It's up to you to comfort him and to let your little pup know that he is going to be happy with you.

FOOD AND WATER BOWLS

Your puppy will need separate bowls for his food and water. Stainless steel pans are generally preferred over plastic bowls, since they sterilize better and pups are less inclined to chew on the metal. Heavy-duty ceramic bowls are popular, but consider how often

TEMPERAMENT ABOVE ALL ELSE

Regardless of breed, a puppy's disposition is perhaps his most important quality. It is, after all, what makes a puppy lovable and "livable." If the puppy's parents or grandparents are known to be snappy or aggressive, the puppy is likely to inherit those tendencies. That can lead to serious problems, such as the dog's becoming a biter, which can lead to eventual abandonment.

you will have to pick up those heavy bowls! Buy adult-sized pans, as your puppy will grow into them before you know it.

THE DOG CRATE

If you think that crates are tools of punishment and confinement for when a dog has misbehaved, think again. Most breeders and almost all

Crates can be purchased at your local pet shop. Top breeders are convinced that crate training is the best way to housebreak and train a Basset Fauve, as well as keep him safe.

PHOTO BY PAULETTE BRAUN

your puppy will adjust to either one, so the choice is up to you. The wire crates offer better visibility for the pup as well as better ventilation. Many of the wire crates easily collapse into suitcase-size carriers. The fiberglass crates, similar to those used by the airlines for animal transport, are sturdier and more den-like. However, the fiberglass crates do not collapse and are less ventilated than a wire crate, which can be problematic in hot weather. Some of the newer crates are made of heavy plastic mesh; they are very lightweight and fold up into slim-line suitcases. However, a mesh crate might not be suitable for a pup with manic chewing habits.

Don't bother with a puppy-sized crate. Although your Basset

trainers recommend a crate as the preferred house-training aid as well as for all-around puppy training and safety. Because dogs are natural den creatures that prefer cave-like environments, the benefits of crate use are many. The crate provides the puppy with his very own "safe house," a cozy place to sleep, take a break or seek comfort with a favorite toy; a travel aid to house your dog when on the road, at motels or at the vet's office; a training aid to help teach your puppy proper toileting habits; a place of solitude when non-dog people happen to drop by and don't want a lively puppy…or even a well-behaved adult dog…saying hello or begging for attention.

Crates come in several types, although the wire crate and the fiberglass airline-type crate are the most popular. Both are safe and

CRATE EXPECTATIONS

To make the crate more inviting to your puppy, you can offer his first meal or two inside the crate, always keeping the crate door open so that he does not feel confined. Keep a favorite toy or two in the crate for him to play with while inside. You can also cover the crate at night with a lightweight sheet to make it more den-like and remove the stimuli of household activity. Never put him in his crate as punishment or as you are scolding him, since he will then associate his crate with negative situations and avoid going there.

Fauve will be a wee fellow when you bring him home, he will grow up in the blink of an eye and your puppy crate will be useless. Purchase a crate that will accommodate an adult Basset Fauve. Adult height ranges from about 12.5 to 15.5 inches at the shoulder when full grown, so a medium-sized crate will fit him nicely.

Bedding and Crate Pads

Your puppy will enjoy some type of soft bedding in his "room" (the crate), something he can snuggle into to feel cozy and secure. Old towels or blankets are good choices for a young pup, since he may (and probably will) have a toileting accident or two in the crate or decide to chew on the bedding material. Once he is fully trained and out of the early chewing stage, you can replace the puppy bedding with a permanent crate pad if you prefer. Crate pads and other dog beds run the gamut from inexpensive to high-end doggie-designer styles, but don't splurge on the good stuff until you are sure that your puppy is reliable and won't tear it up or make a mess on it.

Puppy Toys

Just as infants and other children require objects to stimulate their minds and bodies, puppies need toys to entertain their curious brains, wiggly paws and achy teeth. A fun array of safe doggie toys will help satisfy your puppy's chewing instincts and distract him from gnawing on the leg of your antique chair or your new leather sofa. Most puppy toys are cute and look as if they would be a lot of fun, but not all are

Most anything safe, soft and washable can be used as cozy bedding to line your Basset Fauve's crate.

All in a row, one cuter than the next—how will you choose? Not by looks alone! You must look beyond the puppy appeal to ensure that your chosen pup is sound in health and temperament.

necessarily safe or good for your puppy, so use caution when you go puppy-toy shopping.

Although Bassets Fauves are not known to be voracious chewers like many other dogs, they still love to chew. The best "chewci-fiers" are hard nylon and hard rubber bones, which are safe to gnaw on and come in sizes appropriate for all age groups and breeds. Be especially careful of natural bones, which can splinter or develop dangerous sharp edges; pups can easily swallow or choke on those bone splinters. Veterinarians often tell of surgical nightmares involving bits of splintered bone, because in addition to the danger of choking, the sharp pieces can damage the intestinal tract.

Similarly, rawhide chews, while a favorite of most dogs and puppies, can be equally dangerous. Pieces of rawhide are easily swallowed after they get all gummy from chewing, and dogs have been

known to choke on large pieces of ingested rawhide. Rawhide chews should be offered only when you can supervise the puppy.

Soft woolly toys are special puppy favorites. They come in a wide variety of cute shapes and sizes; some look like little stuffed animals. Puppies love to shake them up and toss them about, or simply carry them around. Be careful of fuzzy toys that have button eyes or noses that your pup could chew off and swallow, and make sure that he does not "disembowel" a squeaky toy to remove the squeaker! Braided rope toys are similar in that they are fun to chew and toss around, but they shred easily and the strings are easy to swallow. The strings are not digestible and, if the puppy doesn't pass them in his stool, he could end up at the vet's office. As with rawhides, your puppy should be closely monitored with rope toys.

If you believe that your pup has ingested one of these forbidden objects, check his stools for the next couple of days to see if he passes them when he defecates. At the same time, also watch for signs of intestinal distress. A call to your veterinarian might be in order to get his advice and be on the safe side.

An all-time favorite toy for puppies (young and old!) is the empty gallon milk jug. Hard plastic juice containers—46 ounces or more—are also excellent. Such containers make lots of noise when they are batted about, and puppies go crazy with delight as they play with them. However, they don't often last very long, so be sure to remove and replace them when they get chewed up on the ends.

A word of caution about homemade toys: be careful with your choices of non-traditional play objects. Never use old shoes or socks, since a puppy cannot distinguish between the old ones on which he's allowed to chew and the new ones in your closet that are strictly off limits. That principle applies to anything that resembles something that you don't want your puppy to chew up.

COLLARS

A lightweight nylon collar is the best choice for a very young pup. Quick-clip collars are easy to put on and remove, and they can be adjusted as the puppy grows. Introduce him to his collar as soon as he comes home to get him accustomed to wearing it. He'll get used to it quickly and won't mind a bit. Make sure that it is snug enough that it won't slip off, yet loose enough to be comfortable for the pup. You should be able to slip two fingers between the collar and his neck. Check the collar often, as puppies grow in spurts and his collar can become too tight almost overnight.

PHOTO BY PAULETTE BRAUN.

TOYS 'R SAFE

The vast array of tantalizing puppy toys is staggering. Stroll through any pet shop or pet-supply outlet and you will see that the choices can be overwhelming. However, not all dog toys are safe or sensible. Most very young puppies enjoy soft woolly toys that they can snuggle with and carry around. (You know they have outgrown them when they shred them up!) Avoid toys that have buttons, tabs or other enhancements that can be chewed off and swallowed. Soft toys that squeak are fun, but make sure your puppy does not disembowel the toy and remove (and swallow) the squeaker. Toys that rattle or make noise can excite a puppy, but they present the same danger as the squeaky kind and so require supervision. Hard rubber toys that bounce can also entertain a pup, but make sure the size of the toy is appropriate to your Basset Fauve.

Leash Life

Dogs love leashes! Believe it or not, most dogs dance for joy every time their owners pick up their leashes. The leash means that the dog is going for a walk—and there are few things more exciting than that! Here are some of the kinds of leashes that are commercially available.

Nylon Leash

Leather Leash

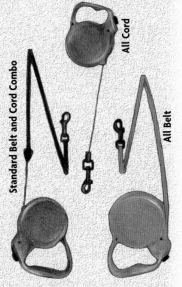

Standard Belt and Cord Combo

All Cord

All Belt

Retractable Leashes

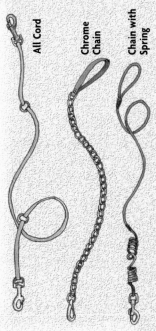

All Cord

Chrome Chain

Chain with Spring

Traditional Leash: Made of cotton, nylon or leather, this is usually about 6 feet in length. A quality-made leather leash is softer on the hands than a nylon one. Durable woven cotton is a popular option. Lengths can vary up to about 48 feet, designed for different uses.

Chain Leash: Usually a metal chain leash with a plastic handle. This is not the best choice for most breeds, as it is heavier than other leashes and difficult to manage.

Retractable Leash: A long nylon cord is housed in a plastic device for extending and retracting. This leash, also known as a flexible leash, is ideal for taking trained dogs for long walks in open areas, although it is not advised for large, powerful breeds. Different lengths and sizes are available, so check that you purchase one appropriate for your dog's weight.

Elastic Leash: A nylon leash with an elastic extension. This is useful for well-trained dogs, especially in conjunction with a head halter. Avoid leashes that are completely elastic, as they afford minimal control to the handler.

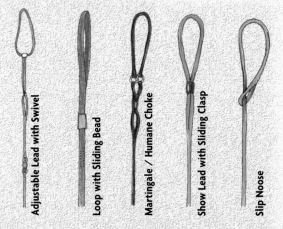

Adjustable Lead with Swivel

Loop with Sliding Bead

Martingale / Humane Choke

Show Lead with Sliding Clasp

Slip Noose

A Variety of Collar-Leash-in-One Products

Adjustable Leash: This has two snaps, one on each end, and several metal rings. It is handy if you need to tether your dog temporarily, but is never to be used with a choke collar.

Tab Leash: A short leash (4 to 6 inches long) that attaches to your dog's collar. This device serves like a handle, in case you have to grab your dog while he's exercising off lead. It's ideal for "half-trained" dogs or dogs that listen only half the time.

Slip Leash: Essentially a leash with a collar built in, similar to what a dog-show handler uses to show a dog. This British-style collar has a ring on the end so that you can form a slip collar. Useful if you have to catch your own runaway dog or a stray.

Choke collars are for training purposes only and should never be used on a puppy under four or five months old.

LEASHES

A 6-foot nylon lead is an excellent choice for a young puppy. It is lightweight and not as tempting to chew as a leather lead. You can switch to a 6-foot leather lead after your pup has grown and is used to walking politely on a lead. For initial puppy walks and house-training purposes, you should invest in a shorter lead so that you have more control over the puppy. At first, you don't want him wandering too far away from you, and when taking him out for toileting you will want to keep him in the specific area chosen for his potty spot.

Once the puppy is heel trained with a traditional leash, you can consider purchasing a retractable lead. A flexible lead is excellent for walking adult dogs that are already leash-wise. The "flexi" allows the dog to roam farther away from you and explore a wider area when out walking, and also retracts when you need to keep him close to you.

HOME SAFETY FOR YOUR PUPPY

The importance of puppy-proofing cannot be overstated. In addition to making your house comfortable for your Basset Fauve's arrival, you also must make sure that your

house is safe for your puppy before you bring him home. There are countless hazards in the owner's personal living environment that a pup can sniff, chew, swallow or destroy. Many are obvious; others are not. Do a thorough advance house check to remove or rearrange those things that could hurt your puppy, keeping any potentially dangerous items out of areas to which he will have access.

Electrical cords are especially dangerous, since puppies view them as irresistible chew toys. Unplug and remove all exposed cords or fasten them beneath a baseboard where the puppy cannot reach them. Veterinarians and firefighters can tell you horror stories about electrical burns and house fires that resulted from puppy-chewed electrical cords.

Give your pup time to acclimate to his new environment. He will familiarize himself with the house and yard (under your watchful eye, of course!) and feel at home in no time.

Consider this a most serious precaution for your puppy and the rest of your family.

Scout your home for tiny objects that might be seen at a pup's eye level. Keep medication bottles and cleaning supplies well out of reach, and do the same with waste baskets and other trash containers. It goes without saying that you should not use rodent poison or other toxic chemicals in any puppy area, and that you must keep such containers safely locked up. You will be amazed at how many places a curious puppy can discover!

Once your house has cleared inspection, check your yard. A sturdy fence, well embedded into the ground, will give your dog a safe place to play and potty. Although Bassets Fauves are not known to be climbers or fence jumpers, they are still athletic

Your Basset Fauve pup will be always on the go, following his curious nose wherever it may lead him, so be sure to stay one step ahead!

dogs, so a 5- to 6-foot-high fence should be adequate to contain an agile youngster or adult. Check the fence periodically for necessary repairs. If there is a weak link or space to squeeze through, you can be sure a determined Basset Fauve will discover it.

The garage and shed can be hazardous places for a pup, as things like fertilizers, chemicals and tools are usually kept there. It's best to keep these areas off limits to the pup. Antifreeze is especially dangerous to dogs, as they find the taste appealing and it only takes a few licks from the driveway to kill a dog, puppy or adult, small breed or large.

VISITING THE VETERINARIAN
A good veterinarian is your Basset Fauve puppy's best health insurance policy. If you do not already have a vet, ask friends and experienced dog people in your area for recommendations so that you can select a vet before you bring your Basset Fauve puppy home. Also arrange for your puppy's first veterinary examination beforehand, since many vets have two- and three-week waiting periods, and your puppy should visit the vet within a day or so of coming home.

It's important to make sure your puppy's first visit to the vet is a pleasant and positive one. The vet should take great care to befriend the pup and handle him gently to make their first meeting a positive experience. The vet will give the pup a thorough physical examination and set up a schedule for vaccinations and other necessary wellness visits. Be sure to show your vet any health and inoculation records which you should have received from your breeder. Your vet is a great source of canine health information, so be sure to ask questions and take notes. Creating a health journal for your puppy will make a handy reference for his wellness and any future health problems that may arise.

SWEETS THAT KILL

Antifreeze would be every dog's favorite topping for a chocolate sundae! However, antifreeze, just like chocolate, kills dogs. That's why you are reading this book and your dog is not planning his own birthday party! Ethylene glycol, found in antifreeze, causes acute renal failure in dogs and can be fatal. Dogs suffering from kidney failure expel little or no urine, act lethargically, may experience vomiting or diarrhea and may resist activity and drinking water. Just a single teaspoon of antifreeze is enough to kill a dog (depending on the size); even for large dogs it only takes a tablespoon or two! Like that irresistible chocolate ice cream, antifreeze is sweet-tasting and smells yummy. Keep it away from your dog!

MEETING THE FAMILY

Your Basset Fauve's homecoming is an exciting time for all members of the family, and it's only natural that everyone will be eager to meet him, pet him and play with him. However, for the puppy's sake, it's best to make these initial family meetings as uneventful as possible so that the pup is not overwhelmed with too much too soon. Remember, he has just left his dam and his littermates and is away from the breeder's home for the first time. Despite his fuzzy wagging tail, he is still apprehensive and wondering where he is and who all these strange humans are. It's best to let him explore on his own and meet the family members as he feels comfortable. Let him investigate all the new smells,

Along with your new puppy come those puppy teeth! For the safety of your pup and your belongings, be sure to puppy-proof and keep anything you don't want chewed out of his reach.

sights and sounds at his own pace. Children should be especially careful to not get overly excited, use loud voices or hug the pup too tightly. Be calm, gentle and affectionate, and be ready to comfort him if he appears frightened or uneasy.

Be sure to show your puppy his new crate during this first day home. Toss a treat or two inside the crate; if he associates the crate with food, he will associate the crate with good things. If he is comfortable with the crate, you can offer him his first meal inside it. Leave the door ajar so he can wander in and out as he chooses.

FIRST NIGHT IN HIS NEW HOME

So much has happened in your Basset Fauve puppy's first day away from the breeder. He had his first car ride to his new home. He's met his new human family and perhaps the other family pets. He has explored his new house and yard, at least those places where he is to be allowed during his first weeks at home. He may have visited his new veterinarian. He has eaten his first meal or two away from his dam and litter-mates. Surely that's enough to tire out an eight-week-old Basset Fauve pup...or so you hope!

It's bedtime. During the day, the pup investigated his crate, which is his new den and sleeping space, so it is not entirely strange to him. Line the crate with a soft towel or blanket that he can snuggle into and gently place him in the crate for the night. Some breeders send home a piece of bedding from where the pup slept with his littermates, and those familiar scents are a great comfort for the puppy on his first night without his siblings.

KEEP OUT OF REACH
Most dogs don't browse around your medicine cabinet, but accidents do happen. The drug acetaminophen, the active ingredient in Tylenol®, can be deadly to dogs and cats if ingested in large quantities. Acetaminophen toxicity, caused by the dog's swallowing 15 to 20 tablets, can be manifested in abdominal pains within a day or two of ingestion, as well as liver damage. If you suspect your dog has swiped a bottle of Tylenol®, get the dog to the vet immediately so that the vet can induce vomiting and cleanse the dog's stomach.

ESTABLISH A ROUTINE

Routine is very important to a puppy's learning environment. To facilitate house-training, use the same exit/entrance door for potty trips and always take the puppy to the same place in the yard. The same principle of consistency applies to all other aspects of puppy training.

He will probably whine or cry. The puppy is objecting to the confinement and the fact that he is alone for the first time. This can be a stressful time for you as well as for the pup. It's important that you remain strong and don't let the puppy out of his crate to comfort him. He will fall asleep eventually. If you release him, the puppy will learn that crying means "out" and will continue that habit. You are laying the groundwork for future habits. Some breeders find that soft music can soothe a crying pup and help him get to sleep.

SOCIALIZING YOUR PUPPY

The next 20 weeks of your Basset Fauve puppy's life are the most important of his entire lifetime. A properly socialized puppy will grow up to be a confident and stable adult who will be a pleasure to live with and a welcome addition to the neighborhood.

The importance of socialization cannot be overemphasized.

Research on canine behavior has proven that puppies who are not exposed to new sights, sounds, people and animals during their first 20 weeks of life will grow up to be timid and fearful, even aggressive, and unable to flourish outside of their home environment.

Socializing your puppy is not difficult and, in fact, will be a fun time for you both. Lead training goes hand in hand with socialization, so your puppy will be learning how to walk on a lead at the same time that he's meeting the neighborhood. Because the Basset Fauve is a such a distinctive breed, your puppy will enjoy being "the new kid on the block." Take him for short walks, to the park and to other dog-friendly places where he will encounter new people, especially children. Puppies automatically recognize children as "little people" and are drawn to play with them. Just

Pups get early life lessons by socializing, playing and interacting with each other, learning the rules of the pack.

An easy way to make friends fast—offer your new puppy something tasty!

confident, responsible dog owner, rightly proud of your handsome Basset Fauve.

Be especially careful of your puppy's encounters and experiences during the eight-to-ten-week-old period, which is also called the "fear period." This is a serious imprinting period, and all contact during this time should be gentle and positive. A frightening or negative event could leave a permanent impression that could affect his future behavior if a similar situation arises.

Also make sure that your puppy has

make sure that you supervise these meetings and that the children do not get too rough or encourage him to play too hard. An overzealous pup can often nip too hard, frightening the child and in turn making the puppy overly excited. A bad experience in puppyhood can impact a dog for life, so a pup that has a negative experience with a child may grow up to be shy or even aggressive around children.

Take your puppy along on your daily errands. Puppies are natural "people magnets," and most people who see your pup will want to pet him. All of these encounters will help to mold him into a confident adult dog. Likewise, you will soon feel like a

THE FAMILY FELINE

A resident cat has feline squatter's rights. The cat will treat the newcomer (your puppy) as he sees fit, regardless of what you do or say. So it's best to let the two of them work things out on their own terms. Cats have a height advantage and will generally leap to higher ground to avoid direct contact with a rambunctious pup. Some will hiss and boldly swat at a pup who passes by or tries to reach the cat. Keep the puppy under control in the presence of the cat and they will eventually become accustomed to each other.

Here's a hint: move the cat's litter box where the puppy can't get into it! It's best to do so well before the pup comes home so the cat is used to the new location.

received his first and second rounds of vaccinations before you expose him to other dogs or bring him to places that other dogs may frequent. Avoid dog parks and other strange-dog areas until your vet assures you that your puppy is fully immunized and resistant to the diseases that can be passed between canines. Discuss socialization with your breeder, as some breeders recommend socializing the puppy even before he has received all his inoculations, depending on how outgoing the breed or puppy may be.

MEET AND MINGLE
Puppies need to meet people and see the world if they are to grow up confident and unafraid. Take your puppy with you on everyday outings and errands. On-lead walks around the neighborhood and to the park offer the pup good exposure to the goings-on of his new human world. Avoid areas frequented by other dogs until your puppy has had his full round of puppy shots; ask your vet when your pup will be properly protected. Arrange for your puppy to meet new people of all ages every week.

LEADER OF THE PUPPY'S PACK

Like other canines, your puppy needs an authority figure, someone he can look up to and regard as the leader of his "pack." His first pack leader was his dam, who taught him to be polite and not chew too hard on her ears or nip at her muzzle. He learned those same lessons from his littermates. If he played too rough, they cried in pain and stopped the game, which sent an important message to the rowdy puppy.

As puppies play together, they are also struggling to determine who will be the boss. Being pack animals, dogs need someone to be in charge. If a litter of puppies remained together beyond puppyhood, one of the pups would emerge as the strongest one, the one who calls the shots.

Once your puppy leaves the pack, he will look intuitively for a new leader. If he does not recognize you as that leader, he will try to assume that position for himself. Of course, it is hard to imagine your adorable Basset Fauve puppy trying to be in charge when he is so small and seemingly helpless. You must remember that these are natural canine instincts. Do not cave in

A puppy kept occupied with safe toys is much less likely to spend his time chewing on things he finds on the ground.

and allow your pup to get the upper "paw."

Just as socialization is so important during these first 20 weeks, so too is your puppy's early education. He was born without any bad habits. He does not know what is good or bad behavior. If he does things like nipping and digging, it's because he is having fun and doesn't know that humans consider these things as "bad." It's your job to teach him proper puppy manners, and this is the best time to accomplish that…before he has developed bad habits, since it is much more difficult to "unlearn" or correct unacceptable learned behavior than to teach good behavior from the start.

Make sure that all members of the family understand the importance of being consistent when training their new puppy. If you tell the puppy to stay off the sofa, and your daughter allows

him to cuddle on the couch to watch her favorite television show, your pup will be confused about what he is and is not allowed to do. Have a family conference before your pup comes home so that everyone understands the basic principles of puppy training and the rules you have set forth for the pup, and agrees to follow them.

The old adage "an ounce of prevention is worth a pound of cure" is especially true when it comes to puppies. It is much easier to prevent inappropriate behavior than it is to change it. It's also easier and less stressful for the pup, since it will keep discipline to a minimum and create a more positive learning environment for him. That, in turn, will also be easier on you.

Here are a few commonsense tips to keep your belongings safe and your puppy out of trouble:

• Keep your closet doors closed and your shoes, socks and other apparel off the floor so your puppy can't get at them.

THE FIRST FAMILY MEETING
Your puppy's first day at home should be quiet and uneventful. Despite his wagging tail, he is still wondering where his mom and siblings are! Let him make friends with other members of the family on his own terms; don't overwhelm him. You have a lifetime ahead to get to know each other.

- Keep a secure lid on the trash container or put the trash where your puppy can't dig into it. He can't damage what he can't reach!
- Supervise your puppy at all times to make sure he is not getting into mischief. If he starts to chew the corner of the rug, you can distract him instantly by tossing a toy for him to fetch. You also will be able to whisk him outside when you notice that he is about to piddle on the carpet. If you can't see your puppy, you can't teach or correct his behavior.

SOLVING PUPPY PROBLEMS

CHEWING AND NIPPING

Nipping at fingers and toes is normal puppy behavior. Chewing is also the way that puppies investigate their surroundings. However, you will have to teach your puppy that chewing anything other than his toys is not acceptable. That won't happen overnight and, at times, puppy teeth will test your patience. However, if you allow nipping and chewing to continue, just think about the damage that a mature Basset Fauve can do with a full set of adult teeth.

Whenever your puppy nips your hand or fingers, cry out "Ouch!" in a loud voice, which should startle your puppy and stop him from nipping, even if only for a moment. Immediately distract him by offering a small treat or an appropriate toy for him to chew instead (which means having chew toys and puppy treats handy or in your pockets at all times). Praise him when he takes the toy and tell him what a good fellow he is. Praise is just as, or even more, important to puppy training as discipline and correction.

Adult dogs enjoy a good chew, too!

Puppies also tend to nip at children more often than adults, since they perceive little ones to be more vulnerable and more similar to their littermates. Teach your children appropriate responses to nipping behavior and, if they are unable to handle it themselves, you may have to intervene. Puppy nips can be quite painful and a child's frightened reaction will only encourage a puppy to nip harder, which is a natural canine response. As with all other puppy situations, interaction between your Basset Fauve puppy and children should be supervised.

Chewing on objects, not just family members' fingers and ankles, is also normal canine behavior that can be especially tedious (for the owner, not the pup) during the teething period when the puppy's adult teeth are coming in. At this stage, chewing just plain feels good. Furniture legs and cabinet corners are common puppy favorites. Shoes and other personal items also taste pretty good to a pup.

The best solution is, once again, prevention. If you value something, keep it tucked away and out of reach. You can't hide your dining-room table in a closet, but you can try to deflect the chewing by applying a bitter product made just to deter dogs from chewing. Available in a spray or cream, this substance is vile-tasting, although safe for dogs, and most puppies will avoid the forbidden object after one tiny taste. You also can apply the product to your leather leash if the puppy tries to chew on his lead during leash-training sessions.

Keep a ready supply of safe chews handy to offer your Basset Fauve as a distraction when he starts to chew on something that's a "no-no." Remember, at this tender age, he does not yet know what is permitted or forbidden, so you have to be "on call" every minute he's awake and on the prowl.

You may lose a treasure or two during puppy's growing-up period, and the furniture could sustain a nasty nick or two. These can be trying times, so be prepared for those inevitable accidents and comfort yourself in knowing that this too shall pass.

JUMPING UP

Although Basset Fauve pups are not known to be notorious jumpers, they are still puppies after all, and puppies jump up...on you, your guests, your counters and your furniture. Just another normal part of growing up, and one you need to meet head-on before it becomes an ingrained habit.

The key to jump correction is consistency. You cannot correct your Basset Fauve for jumping up on you today, then allow it to happen tomorrow by greeting him with hugs and kisses. As you have learned by now, consistency is critical to all puppy lessons.

For starters, try turning your back as soon as the puppy jumps. Jumping up is a means of gaining your attention and, if the pup can't see your face, he may get discouraged and learn that he loses eye contact with his beloved master when he jumps up.

Leash corrections also work, and most puppies respond well to a leash tug if they jump. Grasp the leash close to the puppy's collar and give a quick tug downward, using the command "Off." Do not use the word "Down," since "Down" is used to teach the puppy to lie down, which is a separate action that he will learn during his education in the basic commands. As soon as the puppy has backed off, tell him to sit and immediately praise him for doing so. This will take many repetitions and won't be accomplished quickly, so don't get discouraged or give up...you must be even more persistent than your puppy.

A second method used for jump correction is the spritzer bottle. Fill a spray bottle with water mixed with a bit of lemon juice or vinegar. As soon as puppy jumps, command him "Off" and spritz him with the water mixture. Of course, that means having the

spray bottle handy whenever or wherever jumping usually happens.

Yet a third method to discourage jumping is grasping the puppy's paws and holding them gently but firmly until he struggles to get away. Wait a brief moment or two, then release his paws and give him a command to sit. He should eventually learn that jumping gets him into an uncomfortable predicament.

Children are major victims of puppy jumping, since puppies view little people as ready targets for jumping up as well as nipping. If your children (or their friends) are unable to dispense jump corrections, you will have to intervene and handle it for them.

A pup may jump up on people to say hello, on furniture, to look out a window, to see what's on the coffee table, etc—all instances in which the "Off" command will be helpful.

All puppies enjoy time in the yard, but don't leave your dog outside alone for long periods; he wants to be where you are whenever possible.

Important to prevention is also knowing what you should not do. Never kick your Basset Fauve (for any reason, not just for jumping) or knock him in the chest with your knee. That maneuver could actually harm your puppy. Vets can tell you stories about puppies who suffered broken bones after being banged about when they jumped up.

PUPPY WHINING

Puppies often cry and whine, just as infants and little children do. It's their way of telling us that they are lonely or in need of attention. Your puppy will miss his littermates and will feel insecure when he is left alone. You may be out of the house or just in another room, but he will still feel alone. During these times, the puppy's crate should be his personal comfort station, a place all his own where he can feel safe and secure. Once he learns that being alone is okay and not something to be feared, he will settle down without crying or objecting. You might want to leave a radio on while he is crated, as the sound of human voices can be soothing and will give the impression that people are around.

Give your puppy a favorite cuddly toy or chew toy to entertain him whenever he is crated. You will both be happier: the puppy because he is safe in his den, and you because he is quiet, safe and not getting into puppy escapades that can wreak havoc in your house or cause him danger.

To make sure that your puppy will always view his crate as a safe and cozy place, never, ever, use the crate as punishment. That's the best way to turn the crate into a negative place that the pup will want to avoid. Sure, you can use the crate for your own peace of mind if your puppy is getting into trouble and needs some "time out." Just don't let him know that! Never scold the pup and immediately place him in the crate. Count to ten, give him a couple of hugs and maybe a treat, then scoot him into his crate.

It's also important not to make a big fuss when he is released from the crate. That will make getting out of the crate more appealing than being in the crate, which is just the opposite of what you are trying to achieve.

FOOD GUARDING

Some dogs are picky eaters; others seem to inhale their food without chewing it. Occasionally, the true "chow hound" will become protective of his food, which is one dangerous step toward other aggressive behavior. Food guarding is obvious…your puppy will growl, snarl or even attempt to bite you if you approach his food bowl or put your hand into his pan while he's eating.

This behavior is not acceptable, and very preventable! If your puppy is an especially voracious eater, sit next to him occasionally while he eats and dangle your fingers in his food bowl. Don't feed him in a corner, where he could feel possessive of his eating space. Rather, place his food bowl in an open area of your kitchen where you are in close proximity. Occasionally remove his food in mid-meal, tell him he's a good boy and return his bowl.

If your pup becomes possessive of his food, look for other signs of future aggression, like guarding his favorite toys or refusing to obey obedience commands that he knows. Consult an obedience trainer for help in reinforcing obedience so your Basset Fauve will fully understand that you are the boss.

Growing up, puppies are used to sharing meals with their littermates, so food guarding hopefully will not be a problem when your pup comes to your home.

BASSET FAUVE DE BRETAGNE

VARIETY IS THE SPICE

Although dog-food manufacturers contend that dogs don't like variety in their diets, studies show quite the opposite to be true. Dogs would much rather vary their meals than eat the same old chow day in and day out. Dry kibble is no more exciting for a dog than the same bowl of bran flakes would be for you. Fortunately, there are dozens of varieties available on the market and your dog will likely show preference for certain flavors over others. A word of warning: don't overdo it or you'll develop a fussy eater who turns his nose up at anything other than the finest delicacies.

FEEDING THE BASSET FAUVE

Every Basset Fauve breeder should have his own tried-and-true method of feeding. You can rest assured that along with your puppy will come careful instructions on how to follow the breeder's established feeding program. In the highly unlikely case of the breeder's not automatically providing you with this information, do not leave without asking for it.

What and when you should feed your new puppy will be included in the diet sheet. It is important to understand a specific feeding schedule is important to the puppy's well-being during his crucial growth period. A good rule of thumb to maintain is to gauge the amount you offer at each meal by the amount of food the puppy, or adult for that matter, will eat in five minutes. The recommended content may vary from breeder to breeder, but the five-minute rule is likely to remain constant.

Over-supplementation and forced growth are now looked upon by many breeders as major contributors to the high incidence of skeletal abnormalities and chronic skin conditions found in many pure-bred dogs of the day. Some people may claim these problems are entirely hereditary, but most others feel they can, if nothing more, be exacerbated by diet and overuse of mineral and vitamin supplements for puppies. Therefore, when feeding a commercially prepared dog food, you should add no growth supplements to the Basset Fauve puppy's diet. All leading major-brand dog foods are highly fortified and contain all the nutrients, in proper proportions, that your dog should have. Exceeding this nutrient content can cause nutritional imbalances and both skeletal and joint deformities.

After weaning and on up to about three months, the Basset Fauve puppy should be fed three to four meals a day. From about three months old on, two to three meals a day are sufficient, and by the time the puppy is six months old, he might well be put on a morning/evening schedule. Here again, these are simply rules of thumb. The lean puppy might need a supplemental feeding added to the morning/evening schedule. The too-pudgy puppy should be kept on the two-meal schedule but perhaps be given a bit less at each meal.

A Basset Fauve will usually have reached maximum height by

WEIGHT AND SEE!

When you look at yourself in the mirror each day, you get very used to what you see! It's only when you pull out last year's holiday outfit and can't zipper it that you notice that you've put on some pounds. Dog owners are the same way with their dogs. Often a few pounds go unnoticed, and it's not until some time passes or the vet remarks that your dog looks more than pleasantly plump that you realize what's happened. To avoid your pet's becoming obese right under your very nose, make a habit of routinely evaluating his condition with a hands-on test.

Can you feel, but not see, your dog's rib cage? Does your dog have a waist? His waist should be evident by touch and also visible from above and from the side. In top view, the dog's body should have an hourglass shape. These are indicators of good condition.

While it's not hard to spot an extremely skinny or overly rotund dog, it's the subtle changes that lead up to under- or overweight condition of which we must be aware. If your dog's ribs are visible, he is too thin. Conversely, if you can't feel the ribs under too much fat, and if there's no indication of a waistline, your dog is overweight. Both of these conditions require changes to the diet.

A trip or sometimes just a call to the vet will help you modify your dog's feeding.

Some dogs just love a good meal and they show their appreciation!

dogs get older, their metabolism changes. The older dog usually exercises less, moves more slowly and sleeps more. This change in lifestyle and physiological performance requires a change in diet. Since these changes take place slowly, they might not be recognizable. What is easily recognizable is weight gain. By continuing to feed your dog an

12 to 15 months, but will continue to develop bodily for longer. This can vary according to the type of food used and to the individual dog's bodily development. Bassets Fauves generally can be switched to an adult diet by around 9 to 12 months of age. Major dog-food manufacturers specialize in adult-maintenance food, so it is just necessary for you to pick the one that best suits your dog. For example, very active dogs will have different requirements from sedentary dogs.

The Basset Fauve can be kept on an adult diet until age-related changes necessitate changes in feeding. The breed is considered to have reached "senior citizenship" around ten years of age. As

DIET DON'TS

- Got milk? Don't give it to your dog! Dogs cannot tolerate large quantities of cows' milk, as they do not have the enzymes to digest lactose.
- You may have heard of dog owners' adding raw eggs to their dogs' food for shiny coat or to make the food more palatable, but consumption of raw eggs too often can cause a deficiency of the vitamin biotin.
- Avoid feeding table scraps, as they will upset the balance of the dog's complete food. Additionally, fatty or highly seasoned foods can cause upset canine stomachs.
- Do not offer raw meat to your dog. Raw meat can contain parasites; it also is high in fat.
- Vitamin A toxicity in dogs can be caused by too much raw liver, especially if the dog already gets enough vitamin A in his balanced diet, which should be the case.
- Bones, like chicken, pork-chop and other soft bones, are not suitable as they easily splinter.

adult-maintenance diet when he is slowing down metabolically, he will gain weight. Obesity in an older dog compounds the health problems that already accompany old age.

As your dog gets older, few of his organs function up to par. The kidneys slow down and the intestines become less efficient. These age-related factors are best handled with a change in diet and a change in feeding schedule to give smaller portions that are more easily digested. There is no single best diet for every older dog. While many dogs do well on light or senior diets, other dogs do better on special premium diets such as lamb and rice. Be sensitive to your older Basset Fauve's diet, as this will help control other problems that may arise with your old friend. Many breeders like to lower the protein content for older dogs, and it is generally accepted that a lower protein content is more suitable when a dog has begun to lead a more sedentary life.

Remember that refined sugars are not a part of a canine's natural food acquisition; thus, canine teeth are not genetically disposed to handling these sugars. Do not feed your Basset Fauve sugar products and avoid products that contain sugar in any high degree. Be cautious of "people foods" that are potentially lethal to dogs, such as chocolate and onions.

NOT HUNGRY?
No dog in his right mind would turn down his dinner, would he? If you notice that your dog has lost interest in his food, there could be any number of causes. Dental problems are a common cause of appetite loss, one that is often overlooked. If your dog has a toothache, a loose tooth or sore gums from infection, chances are it doesn't feel so good to chew. Think about when you've had a toothache! If your dog does not approach the food bowl with his usual enthusiasm, look inside his mouth for signs of a problem. Whatever the cause, you'll want to consult your vet so that your chow hound can get back to his happy, hungry self as soon as possible.

Fresh water and a properly prepared balanced diet that contains the essential nutrients in correct proportions are all a healthy Basset Fauve needs to be offered. Dog foods come in many types: canned, dry, semi-moist,

dog at all times. There are special circumstances, such as during puppy housebreaking, when you will want to monitor your pup's water intake so that you will be able to predict when he will need to relieve himself, but water must be available to him nonetheless. Water is essential for hydration and proper body function just as it is in humans.

You will get to know how much your dog typically drinks in a day. Of course, in the heat or if

Fresh clean water, made available to the dog at all times, is just as important to your dog's health as the nutrients in his food.

"scientifically fortified," "all-natural" and so on. A visit to your local supermarket or pet store will reveal how vast an array you will be able to select from. Bassets Fauves de Bretagne are generally not fussy eaters, so they are not especially difficult to feed. Actually, they have rather a reputation for eating anything available! Again, a carefully selected breeder should be able to give good advice regarding the diet that has suited his or her own dogs best. As your Fauve will most probably enjoy his food, take care not to allow him to put on too much weight, especially in old age.

DON'T FORGET THE WATER!

For a dog, it's always time for a drink! Regardless of what type of food he eats, there's no doubt that he needs plenty of water. Fresh cold water, in a clean bowl, should be freely available to your

SWITCHING FOODS

There are certain times in a dog's life when it becomes necessary to switch his food; for example, from puppy to adult food and then from adult to senior-dog food. Additionally, you may decide to feed your pup a different type of food from what he received from the breeder, and there may be "emergency" situations in which you can't find your dog's normal brand and have to offer something else temporarily. Anytime a change is made, for whatever reason, the switch must be done gradually. You don't want to upset the dog's stomach or end up with a picky eater who refuses to eat something new. A tried-and-true approach is, over the course of about a week, to mix a little of the new food in with the old, increasing the proportion of new to old as the days progress. At the end of the week, you'll be feeding his regular portions of the new food, and he will barely notice the change.

exercising vigorously, he will be more thirsty and will drink more. However, if he begins to drink noticeably more water for no apparent reason, this could signal any of various problems, and you are advised to consult your vet.

Water is the best drink for dogs. Some owners are tempted to give milk from time to time or to moisten dry food with milk, but dogs do not have the enzymes necessary to digest the lactose in milk, which is much different from the milk that nursing puppies receive. Therefore, stick with clean fresh water to quench your dog's thirst, and always have it readily available to him.

EXERCISE

The Basset Fauve loves exercise and should be allowed some free running each day in a safe area. Although this breed will be more than happy to get plenty of exercise, a moderate amount daily will suffice if that suits your lifestyle. This is a breed that seems ready to accept any amount of exercise, but also enjoys relaxing in front of the fire at home. He is an active little dog that needs a fair amount of exercise daily, but is equally happy to spend quiet time in the home.

Because the Basset Fauve has such a good nose, it is important to begin training as early as possible, especially the recall exercise, meaning that the dog

comes to you reliably when called. If a Fauve picks up an interesting scent, he will follow his nose which, after all, is what he was bred for! That being said, free runs should, of course, only be allowed in places that are securely enclosed. All possible escape routes should be thoroughly checked out before letting your Basset Fauve off lead.

Just as with anything else you do with your dog, you must set a routine for his exercise. It's the same as your daily morning run before work or never missing the 7 p.m. aerobics class. If you plan it and get into the habit of actually doing it, it will become just another part of your day. Think of it as making daily exercise appointments with your dog, and stick to your schedule.

As a rule, dogs in normal health should have at least a half-hour of activity each day. Dogs with health or orthopedic problems may have specific limita-

This smiling Basset Fauve is happy to go for a good run and stretch his little legs.

Don't overdo it with your young Basset Fauve's exercise. Puppies get plenty of activity just being puppies!

tions and their exercise plans are best devised with the help of a vet. For healthy dogs, there are many ways to fit 30 minutes of activity into your day. Depending on your schedule, you may plan a 15-minute walk and activity session in the morning and again in the evening, or do it all at once in a half-hour session each day. Walking is the most popular way to exercise a dog (it's good for you, too!); other suggestions include retrieving games, jogging and Frisbee® or other active games with his toys. If you have a safe body of water nearby and a dog that likes to swim, swimming is an excellent form of exercise for dogs, putting no stress on his frame.

On that note, some precautions should be taken with a puppy's exercise. During his first year, when he is growing and developing, he should not be subject to strenuous activity that stresses his body. Short walks at a comfortable pace and play sessions in the yard are good for a growing pup, and his exercise can be increased as he grows up.

For overweight dogs, dietary changes and activity will help the goal of weight loss. (Sound familiar?) While they should of course be encouraged to be active, remember not to overdo it, as the excess weight is already putting strain on his vital organs and bones. As for active and working dogs, some of them never seem to tire! They will enjoy time spent with their owners doing things together.

After exercise, any dog should be allowed to settle down quietly for a rest. It is essential to remember that no dog should be fed within at least an hour (before or after) of strenuous exercise.

Regardless of your dog's condition and activity level, exercise offers benefits to all dogs and owners. Consider the fact that dogs who are kept active are more stimulated both physically and mentally, meaning that they are less likely to become bored and lapse into destructive behavior. Also consider the benefits of one-on-one time with your dog every day, continually strengthening the bond between the two of you. Furthermore, exercising together will improve health and longevity for both of you. You need exercise, and now you both have a workout partner and motivator!

GROOMING

BRUSHING

In order to keep a Basset Fauve's harsh, dense coat in good, healthy, clean condition, some grooming is essential. Every owner will have his or her own preference as to what equipment suits best, but the basic items include a slicker brush and a strong metal comb. Although the coat does not require a great deal of attention, it is wise to get into the routine of grooming regularly. Many people like to strip out their Fauve's coat about twice a year.

In between brushing sessions, pay attention to your Fauve's coat and make sure that he hasn't picked up debris in his coat when outdoors. Use grooming time to check his skin for any lumps, bumps, insects or other abnormalities. A Basset Fauve that has become wet when exercising in the rain should always be wiped down thoroughly with a towel so as not to remain damp, special attention being paid to the underside.

BATHING

In general, dogs need to be bathed only a few times a year, possibly more often if your dog gets into something messy or if he starts to smell like a dog. Show dogs are usually bathed before every show, which could be as frequent as weekly, although this depends on the owner. Bathing too frequently can have negative effects on the skin and coat, removing natural oils and causing dryness.

If you give your dog his first bath when he is young, he will become accustomed to the process. Wrestling a dog into the tub or chasing a freshly shampooed dog who has escaped from the bath will be no fun! Most dogs don't naturally enjoy their baths, but you at least want them to cooperate with you.

Before bathing the dog, have the items you'll need close at hand. First, decide where you will bathe the dog. You should have a tub or basin with a non-slip surface. Small dogs can even be bathed in a sink. In warm weather, some like to use a

The Basset Fauve is not a high-maintenance breed in terms of grooming, but his harsh coat does require some special attention to keep its correct texture.

portable pool in the yard, although you'll want to make sure your dog doesn't head for the nearest dirt pile following his bath! You will also need a hose or shower spray to wet the coat thoroughly, a shampoo formulated for dogs, absorbent towels and perhaps a blow dryer. Human shampoos are too harsh for dogs' coats and will dry them out.

Before wetting the dog, give him a brush-through to remove any dead hair, dirt and mats. Make sure he is at ease in the tub and have the water at a comfortable temperature. Begin bathing by wetting the coat all the way down to the skin. Massage in the shampoo, keeping it away from

his face and eyes. Rinse him thoroughly, again avoiding the eyes and ears, as you don't want to get water in the ear canals. A thorough rinsing is important, as shampoo residue is drying and itchy to the dog. After rinsing, wrap him in a towel to absorb the initial moisture. You can finish drying with either a towel or a blow dryer on low heat, held at a safe distance from the dog. You should keep the dog indoors and away from drafts until he is completely dry.

NAIL CLIPPING

Having their nails trimmed is not on many dogs' lists of favorite things to do. With this in mind,

A metal comb can be used over the whole body to remove dead hair, dust and debris that can collect in the coat and cause matting.

This grooming glove has rubber knobs to brush and massage the dog on one side, and a smooth cloth on the other side for the finishing touches. Most dogs love the feel of the grooming glove—it's just like being petted.

you will need to accustom your puppy to the procedure at a young age so that he will sit still (well, as still as he can) for his pedicures. Long nails can cause the dog's feet to spread, which is not good for him; likewise, long nails can hurt if they unintentionally scratch, not good for you!

Some dogs' nails are worn down naturally by regular walking on hard surfaces, so the frequency with which you clip depends on your individual dog. Look at his nails from time to time and clip as needed; a good way to know when it's time for a trim is if you hear your dog clicking as he walks across the floor.

There are several types of nail clippers and even electric nail-grinding tools made for dogs; first we'll discuss using the clipper. To start, have your clipper ready and some doggie treats on hand. You want your pup to view his nail-clipping sessions in a positive light, and what better way to convince him than with food? You may want to enlist the help of an assistant to comfort the pup and offer treats as you concentrate on the clipping itself. The guillotine-type clipper is thought of by many as the easiest type to use; the nail tip is inserted into the opening and blades on the top and bottom snip it off in one clip.

Start by grasping the pup's paw; a little pressure on the foot pad causes the nail to extend, making it easier to clip. Clip off a

you do not want to cut into the quick. On that note, if you do cut the quick, which will cause bleeding, you can stem the flow of blood with a styptic pencil or other clotting agent. If you mistakenly nip the quick, do not panic or fuss, as this will cause the pup to be afraid. Simply reassure the pup, stop the bleeding and move on to the next nail. Don't be discouraged; you will become a professional canine pedicurist with practice.

You may or may not be able to see the quick, so it's best to just clip off a small bit at a time. If

Don't neglect any areas of the dog. The feathering on the legs should be combed through, as these areas are prone to matting and picking up debris from outside.

little at a time. If you can see the "quick," which is a blood vessel that runs through each nail, you will know how much to trim, as

---

SELECTING THE RIGHT BRUSHES AND COMBS

Will a curry comb make my dog look slicker? Is a rake smaller than a pin brush? Do I choose nylon or natural bristles? Buying a dog brush can make the hairs on your head stand on end! Here's a quick once-over to educate you on the different types of brushes.

• **Slicker Brush:** Fine metal prongs closely set on a curved base. Used to remove dead coat from the undercoat of medium- to long-coated breeds.

• **Pin Brush:** Metal pins, often covered with rubber tips, set on an oval base. Used to remove shedding hair and is gentler than a slicker brush.

• **Metal Comb:** Steel teeth attached to a steel handle; the closeness and size of the teeth varies greatly. A "flea comb" has tiny teeth set very closely together and is used to find fleas in a dog's coat. Combs with wider teeth are used for detangling longer coats.

• **Rake:** Long-toothed comb with a short handle. Used to remove undercoat from heavily coated breeds with dense undercoats.

• **Soft-bristle Brush:** Nylon or natural bristles set in a plastic or wood base. Used on short coats or long coats (without undercoats).

• **Rubber Brush:** Rubber prongs, with or without a handle. Used for short-coated dogs. Good for use during shampooing.

• **Combination Brushes:** Two-sided brush with a different type of surface on each side; for example, pin brush on one side and slicker on the other, or bristle brush on one side and pin brush on the other. An economical choice if you need two kinds of brushes.

• **Grooming Glove:** Sometimes called a hound glove, used to give sleek-coated dogs a once-over.

you see a dark dot in the center of the nail, this is the quick and your cue to stop clipping. Tell the puppy he's a "good boy" and offer a piece of treat with each nail. You can also use nail-clipping time to examine the footpads, making sure that they are not dry and cracked and that nothing has become embedded in them.

The nail grinder, the second choice, is many owners' first choice. Accustoming the puppy to the sound of the grinder and sensation of the buzz presents fewer challenges than the clipper, and there's no chance of cutting through the quick. Use the grinder on a low setting and always talk soothingly to your dog. He won't mind his salon visit, and he'll have nicely polished nails as well.

EAR CLEANING

While keeping your dog's ears clean unfortunately will not cause him to "hear" your commands any better, it will protect him from ear infection and ear-mite infestation. In addition, a dog's ears are vulnerable to waxy build-up and to collecting foreign matter from the outdoors. Look in your dog's ears regularly to ensure that they look pink, clean and otherwise healthy. Even if they

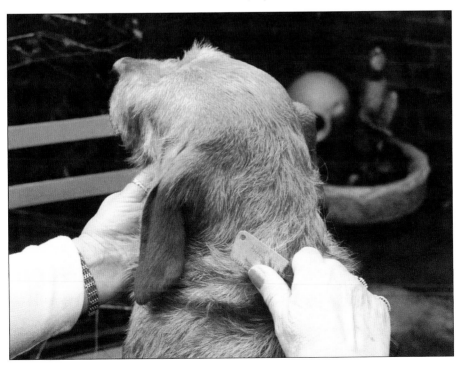

Hand stripping requires some practice, but it's a skill that an owner can learn and is necessary to preserve the desired harsh texture of the Basset Fauve's coat.

Nail trimming is never a dog's favorite part of the grooming routine, but a dog who has had his nails trimmed from a young age will be used to the procedure and should tolerate it without any fuss.

look fine, an odor in the ears signals a problem and means it's time to call the vet.

A dog's ears should be cleaned regularly; once a week is suggested, and you can do this along with your regular brushing. Using a cotton ball or pad, and never probing into the ear canal, wipe the ear gently. You can use an ear-cleansing liquid or powder available from your vet or pet-supply store; some owners prefer to use home-made solutions with ingredients like one part white vinegar and one part hydrogen peroxide. Ask your vet about

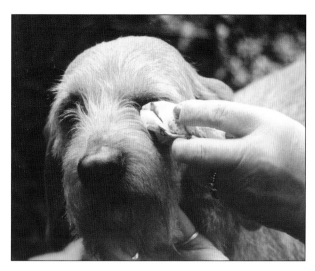

home remedies before you attempt to concoct something on your own!

Keep your dog's ears free of excess hair by plucking it as needed. If done gently, this will be painless for the dog. Look for wax, brown droppings (a sign of ear mites), redness or any other abnormalities. At the first sign of a problem, contact your vet so that he can prescribe an appropriate medication.

Areas around the eyes are easily cleaned with a soft wipe and a cleansing solution made for this purpose, which should be available at your local pet shop.

EYE CARE

During grooming sessions, pay extra attention to the condition of your dog's eyes. If the area around the eyes is soiled or if tear staining has occurred, there are various cleaning agents made especially for this purpose. Look at the dog's eyes to make sure no debris has entered; dogs with large eyes and those who spend

---

THE EARS KNOW

Examining your puppy's ears helps ensure good internal health. The ears are the eyes to the dog's innards! Begin handling your puppy's ears when he's still young so that he doesn't protest every time you lift a flap or touch his ears. Yeast and bacteria are two of the culprits that you can detect by examining the ear. You will notice a strong, often foul, odor, debris, redness or some kind of discharge. All of these point to health problems that can worsen over time. Additionally, you are on the lookout for wax accumulation, ear mites and other tiny bothersome parasites and their even tinier droppings. You may have to pluck hair with tweezers in order to have a better view into the dog's ears, but this is painless if done carefully.

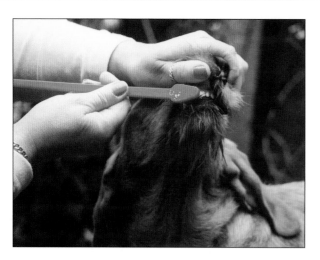

dental problems by two years of age, and the percentage is higher in older dogs. Therefore it is highly likely that your dog will have trouble with his teeth and gums unless you are proactive with home dental care.

The most common dental problem in dogs is plaque build-up. If not treated, this causes gum disease, infection and resultant tooth loss. Bacteria from these infections spread throughout the body, affecting the vital organs. Do you need much more convincing to start brushing your

time outdoors are especially prone to this.

The signs of an eye infection are obvious: mucus, redness, puffiness, scabs or other signs of irritation. If your dog's eyes become infected, the vet will likely prescribe an antibiotic ointment for treatment. If you notice signs of more serious problems, such as opacities in the eye, which usually indicate cataracts, consult the vet at once. Taking time to pay attention to your dog's eyes will alert you in the early stages of any problem so that you can get your dog treatment as soon as possible. You could save your dog's sight!

A CLEAN SMILE

Another essential part of grooming is brushing your dog's teeth and checking his overall oral condition. Studies show that around 80% of dogs experience

WATER SHORTAGE

No matter how well behaved your dog is, bathing is always a project! Nothing can substitute for a good warm bath, but owners do have the option of giving their dogs "dry" baths. Pet shops sell excellent products, in both powder and spray forms, designed for spot-cleaning your dog. These dry shampoos are convenient for touch-up jobs when you don't have the time to bathe your dog in the traditional way.

Muddy feet, messy behinds and smelly coats can be spot-cleaned and deodorized with a "wet-nap"-style cleaner. On those days when your dog insists on rolling in fresh goose droppings and there's no time for a bath, a spot bath can save the day. These pre-moistened wipes are also handy for other grooming needs like wiping faces, ears and eyes and freshening tails and behinds.

dog's teeth? If so, take a good whiff of your dog's breath, and read on.

Fortunately, home dental care is rather easy and convenient for pet owners. Specially formulated canine toothpaste is easy to find. You should use one of these, not a product for humans. Some doggie pastes are even available in flavors appealing to dogs. If he likes the flavor, he will tolerate the process better, making things much easier for you! Doggie toothbrushes come in different sizes and are designed to fit the contour of a canine mouth. Rubber fingertip brushes fit right on one of your fingers and have rubber nodes to clean the teeth and massage the gums. This may be easier to handle, as it is akin to rubbing your dog's teeth with your finger.

As with other grooming tasks, accustom your pup to his dental care early on. Start gently, for a few minutes at a time, so that he gets used to the feel of the brush and to your handling his mouth. Offer praise and petting so that he looks at tooth-care time as a time when he gets extra love and attention. The routine should ideally become second nature; the minimum is that he at least tolerate it.

Aside from brushing, offer dental toys to your dog and feed crunchy biscuits, which help to minimize plaque. Rope toys have

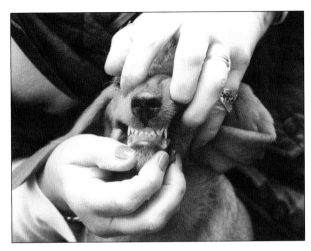

This puppy's off to a good start with a healthy bite.

the added benefit of acting like floss as the dog chews. At your adult dog's yearly check-ups, the vet will likely perform a thorough tooth scraping as well as a complete check for any problems. Proper care of your dog's teeth will ensure that you will enjoy your dog's smile for many years to come. The next time your dog goes to give you a hello kiss, you'll be glad you spent the time caring for his teeth.

THE OTHER END

Dogs sometime have troubles with their anal glands, which are sacs located beside the anal vent. These should empty when a dog has normal bowel movements but, if not, they can become full or impacted, causing discomfort for a dog. Owners often are alarmed to see their dogs scooting across the floor, dragging their behinds behind!

This is a dog's attempt to empty the glands himself.

Some brave owners attempt to evacuate their dogs' anal glands themselves during grooming, but no one will tell you that this is a pleasant task! Thus, many owners prefer to make the trip to the vet to have the vet take care of the problem; others whose dogs visit a groomer can have this done by the groomer if he offers this as part of his services. Regardless, don't neglect the dog's other end in your home-care routine and look for scooting, licking or other signs of discomfort "back there" to ascertain if the anal glands need to be emptied.

IDENTIFICATION AND TRAVEL

ID FOR YOUR DOG

You love your dog and want to keep him safe. Of course you take every precaution to prevent his escaping from the yard or becoming lost or stolen. You have a sturdy high fence and you always keep your dog on lead when out and about in public places. However, if your dog is not properly identified, you are overlooking a major aspect of his safety. We hope to never be in a situation where our dog is missing, but we should practice prevention in the unfortunate case that this happens; identification greatly increases the chances of your dog's being returned to you.

There are several ways to identify your dog. First, the traditional dog tag should be a staple in your dog's wardrobe, attached to his everyday collar. Tags can be made of sturdy plastic and various metals, and should include your contact information so that a person who finds the dog can get in touch with you right away to arrange his return. Many people today enjoy the wide range of decorative tags available, so have fun and create a tag to match your dog's personality. Of course, it is important that the tag stays on the collar, so have a secure "O" ring attachment; you also can explore the type of tag that slides right onto the collar.

In addition to the ID tag, which every dog should wear even if identified by another method, two other forms of identification have become popular:

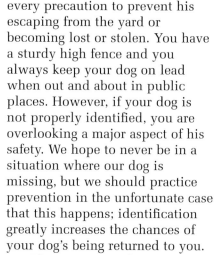

PET OR STRAY?
Besides the obvious benefit of providing your contact information to whomever finds your lost dog, an ID tag makes your dog more approachable and more likely to be recovered. A strange dog wandering the neighborhood without a collar and tags will look like a stray, while the collar and tags indicate that the dog is someone's pet. Even if the ID tags become detached from the collar, the collar alone will make a person more likely to pick up the dog.

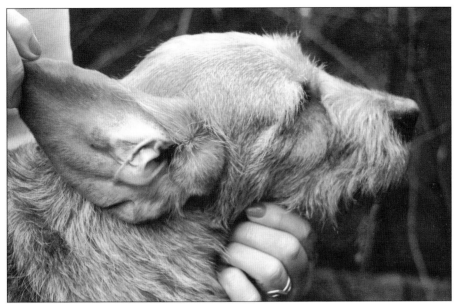

The light-colored skin inside the ear makes a tattoo easily visible; this is the most common area on which ID tattoos are done.

microchipping and tattooing. In microchipping, a tiny scannable chip is painlessly inserted under the dog's skin. The number is registered to you so that, if your lost dog turns up at a clinic or shelter, the chip can be scanned to retrieve your contact information.

The advantage of the microchip is that it is a permanent form of ID, but there are some factors to consider. Several different companies make microchips, and not all are compatible with the others' scanning devices. It's best to find a company with a universal microchip that can be read by scanners made by other companies as well. It won't do any good to have the dog chipped if the information cannot be

retrieved. Also, not every humane society, shelter and clinic is equipped with a scanner, although more and more facilities are equipping themselves. In fact, many shelters microchip dogs that they adopt out to new homes.

In the US, there are five or six major microchip manufacturers as well as a few databases. The American Kennel Club's Companion Animal Recovery unit works in conjunction with HomeAgain™ Companion Animal Retrieval System (Schering-Plough). In the UK, The Kennel Club is affiliated with the National Pet Register, operated by Wood Green Animal Shelters.

Because the microchip is not visible to the eye, the dog must wear a tag that states that he is

A safety gate can be used to partition the back section of a station wagon, SUV or van to create an area of secure confinement for your dog during travel.

microchipped so that whoever picks him up will know to have him scanned. He of course also should have a tag with contact information in case his chip cannot be read. Humane societies and veterinary clinics offer this service, which is usually very affordable.

Though less popular than microchipping, tattooing is another permanent method of ID for dogs. Most vets perform this service, and there are also clinics that perform dog tattooing. This is also an affordable procedure and

one that will not cause much discomfort for the dog. It is best to put the tattoo in a visible area, such as the ear, to deter theft. It is sad to say that there are cases of dogs' being stolen and sold to research laboratories, but such laboratories will not accept tattooed dogs.

To ensure that the tattoo is effective in aiding your dog's return to you, the tattoo number must be registered with a national organization. That way, when someone finds a tattooed dog, a phone call to the registry will quickly match the dog with his owner.

HIT THE ROAD

Car travel with your dog may be limited to necessity only, such as trips to the vet, or you may bring your dog along most everywhere you go. This will depend much on your individual dog and how he reacts to rides in the car. You can begin desensitizing your dog to car travel as a pup so that it's something that he's used to. Still, some dogs suffer from motion sickness. Your vet may prescribe a medication for this if trips in the car pose a problem for your dog. At the very least, you will need to get him to the vet, so he will need to tolerate these trips with the least amount of hassle possible.

Start taking your pup on short trips, maybe just around the block to start. If he is fine with short trips, lengthen your rides a little at a time. Start to take him on your errands or just for drives around town. By this time it will be easy to tell if your dog is a born traveler or if he will prefer staying at home when you are on the road.

Of course, safety is a concern for dogs in the car. First, he must travel securely, not left loose to roam about the car where he could be injured or distract the driver. A young pup can be held by a passenger initially but should soon graduate to a travel crate, which can be the same crate he uses in the home. Other options include a car harness (like a seat belt for dogs) and partitioning the back of the car with a gate made for this purpose.

Bring along what you will need for the dog. He should wear his collar and ID tags, of course, and you should bring his leash, water (and food if a long trip) and clean-up materials for potty breaks and in case of motion sickness. Always keep your dog on his leash when you make stops, and never leave him alone in the car. Many a dog has died from the heat inside a closed car; this does not take much time at all. A dog left alone inside a car can also be a target for thieves.

UP, UP AND AWAY!

Taking a trip by air does not mean that your dog cannot accompany you, it just means that you will have to be well informed and well prepared. The majority of dogs travel as checked cargo; only the smallest of breeds are allowed in the cabin with their owners. Your dog must travel in an airline-approved travel crate appropriate to his size so that he will be safe and comfortable during the flight. If the crate that you use at home does not meet the airline's specifications, you can purchase one from the airline or from your pet-supply store (making sure it is labeled as airline-approved).

It's best to have the crate in advance of your trip to give the dog time to get accustomed to it. You can put a familiar blanket and a favorite toy or two in the crate with the dog to make him feel at home and to keep him occupied. The crate should be lined with absorbent material for the trip, with bowls for food and water attached to the outside of the crate. The crate must be labeled with your contact information, feeding instructions and a statement asserting that the dog was fed within a certain time frame of arrival at the airport (check with your airline). You will also have to provide proof of current vaccinations.

Again, advance planning is the key to smooth sailing in the skies. Make your reservations well ahead of time and know what restrictions your airline imposes: no travel during certain months, refusal of certain breeds, restrictions on certain destinations. In spite of all of these variables, major carriers have much experience with transporting animals, so have a safe flight!

DOG-FRIENDLY DESTINATIONS
When planning vacations, a question that often arises is, "Who will watch the dog?" More and more families, however, are answering that question with, "We will!" With the rise in dog-friendly places to visit, the number of families who bring their dogs along on vacation is on the rise. A search online for dog-friendly vacations will turn up many choices, as well as resources for owners of canine travelers. Ask others for suggestions: your vet, your breeder, other dog owners, breed club members, people at the local doggie day care.

Traveling with your dog means providing for his comfort and safety, and you will have to pack a bag for him just as you do for yourself (although you probably won't have liver treats in your own suitcase!). Bring his everyday items: food, water, bowls, leash and collar (with ID), brush and comb, toys, bed, crate, plus any additional accessories that he will need once you get to your vacation spot. If he takes medication, don't forget to bring it with you. If going camping or on another type of outdoor excursion, take precautions to protect your dog from ticks, mosquitoes and other pests. Above all, have a good time with your dog and enjoy each other's company!

BOARDING
Today there are many options for dog owners who need someone to care for their dogs in certain circumstances. While many think of boarding their dogs as something to do when away on vacation, many others use the

services of doggie "daycare" facilities, dropping their dogs off to spend the day while they are at work. Many of these facilities offer both long-term and daily care. Many go beyond just boarding and cater to all sorts of needs, with on-site grooming, veterinary care, training classes and even "web-cams" where owners can log onto the Internet and check out what their dogs are up to. Most dogs enjoy the activity and time spent with other dogs.

Before you need to use such a service, check out the ones in your area. Make visits to see the facilities, meet the staff, discuss fees and available services and see if this is a place where you think your dog will be happy. It is best to do your research in advance so that you're not stuck at the last minute, forced to make a rushed decision without knowing if the kennel that you've chosen meets your standards. You also can check with your vet's office to see if they offer boarding for their clients or if they can recommend a good kennel in the area.

The kennel will need to see proof of your dog's health records and vaccinations so as not to spread illness from dog to dog. Your dog also will need proper identification. Owners usually experience some separation anxiety the first time they have to leave their dog in someone else's care, so it's reassuring to know that the kennel you choose is run by experienced, caring, true dog people.

Research the boarding facilities in your area and take the time to visit a few so that you'll have a suitable kennel in mind when the need arises to board your dog.

BASSET FAUVE DE BRETAGNE

Training won't work if your pup is bent on exploring or other distractions, so you might want to begin your lessons indoors and then progress to outdoors once he's begun to learn the commands.

BASIC TRAINING PRINCIPLES: PUPPY VS. ADULT

There's a big difference between training an adult dog and training a young puppy. With a young puppy, everything is new! At eight to ten weeks of age, he will be experiencing many things, and he has nothing to which to compare these experiences. Up to this point, he has been with his dam and littermates, not one-on-one with people except in his interactions with his breeder and visitors to the litter.

When you first bring the Basset Fauve puppy home, he is eager to please you. This means that he accepts doing things your way. During the next couple of months, he will absorb the basis of everything he needs to know for the rest of his life. This early age is even referred to as the "sponge" stage. After that, for the next 18 months, it's up to you to reinforce good manners by building on the foundation that you've established. Once your puppy is reliable in basic commands and behavior, and has reached the appropriate age, you may gradually introduce him to some of the interesting sports, games and activities available to pet owners and their dogs.

Raising your puppy is a family affair. Each member of the

"SCHOOL" MODE
When is your puppy ready for a lesson? Maybe not always when you are. Attempting training with treats just before his mealtime is asking for disaster. Notice what times of day he performs best and make that Fido's school time.

family must know what rules to set forth for the puppy and how to use the same one-word commands to mean exactly the same thing every time. Even if yours is a large family, one person will soon be considered by the pup to be the leader, the Alpha person in his pack, the "boss" who must be obeyed. Often that highly regarded person turns out to be the one who feeds the puppy. Food ranks very high on the puppy's list of important things! That's why your puppy is rewarded with small treats along with verbal praise when he responds to you correctly. As the puppy learns to do what you want him to do, the food rewards are gradually eliminated and only the praise remains. If you were to keep up with the food treats, you could have two problems on your hands—an obese dog and a beggar.

The Basset Fauve de Bretagne is a bright and eager student, ready to learn!

BOOT CAMP

Even if one member of the family assumes the role of "drill sergeant," every member of the family has to know what's involved in the dog's education. Success depends on consistency and knowing what words to use, how to use them, how to say them and, most important to the dog, how to praise. The dog will be happy to respond to all members of the family, but don't make the little guy think he's in boot camp!

Training begins the minute your Basset Fauve steps through the doorway of your home, so don't make the mistake of putting the puppy on the floor and telling him by your actions, "Go for it! Run wild!" Even if this is your first puppy, you must act as if you know what you're doing: be the boss. An uncertain pup may be terrified to move, while a bold one will be ready to take you at your word and start plotting to destroy the house! Before you collected your puppy, you decided where his own special place would be, and that's where to put him when you first arrive home. Give him a house tour after he has investigated his area and had a nap and a bathroom "pit stop."

It's worth mentioning here that if you've adopted an adult

Training goes beyond sit and stay, it also means teaching the house rules, which you must decide on and enforce. One such rule is: will your dog be allowed on the furniture?

dog that is completely trained to your liking, lucky you! You're off the hook! However, if that dog spent his life up to this point in a kennel, or even in a good home but without any real training, be prepared to tackle the job ahead. A dog three years of age or older with no previous training cannot be blamed for not knowing what he was never taught. While the dog is trying to understand and learn your rules, at the same time he has to unlearn many of his previously self-taught habits and general view of the world.

Working with a professional trainer will speed up your progress with an adopted adult dog. You'll need patience, too. Some new rules may be close to

impossible for the dog to accept. After all, he's been successful so far by doing everything his way! (Patience again.) He may agree with your instruction for a few days and then slip back into his old ways, so you must be just as consistent and understanding in your teaching as you would be with a puppy. (More patience needed yet again!) Your dog has to learn to pay attention to your voice, your family, the daily routine, new smells, new sounds and, in some cases, even a new climate.

One of the most important things to find out about a newly adopted adult dog is his reaction to children (yours and others), strangers and your friends, and how he acts upon meeting other dogs. If he was not socialized with dogs as a puppy, this could be a major problem. This does not

LEADER OF THE PACK

Canines are pack animals. They live according to pack rules, and every pack has only one leader. Guess what? That's you! To establish your position of authority, lay down the rules and be fair and good-natured in all your dealings with your dog. He will consider young children as his littermates, but the one who trains him, who feeds him, who grooms him, who expects him to come into line, that's his leader. And he who leads must be obeyed.

mean that he's a "bad" dog, a vicious dog or an aggressive dog; rather, it means that he has no idea how to read another dog's body language. There's no way for him to tell if the other dog is a friend or foe. Survival instinct takes over, telling him to attack first and ask questions later. This definitely calls for professional help and, even then, may not be a behavior that can be corrected 100% reliably (or even at all). If you have a puppy, this is why it is so very important to introduce your young puppy properly to other puppies and "dog-friendly" adult dogs.

HOUSE-TRAINING

Dogs are tactile creatures when it comes to house-training. In other words, they respond to the surface on which they are given approval to eliminate. The choice is yours (the dog's version is in parentheses): The lawn (including the neighbors' lawns)? A bare patch of earth under a tree (where people like to sit and relax in the summertime)? Concrete steps or patio (all sidewalks, garage and basement floors)? The curbside (watch out for cars)? A small area of crushed stone in a corner of the yard (mine!)? The latter is the best choice if you can manage it, because it will remain strictly for the dog's use and is easy to keep clean.

DAILY SCHEDULE
How many relief trips does your puppy need per day? A puppy up to the age of 14 weeks will need to go outside about 8 to 12 times per day! You will have to take the pup out any time he starts sniffing around the floor or turning in small circles, as well as after naps, meals, games and lessons or whenever he's released from his crate. Once the puppy is 14 to 22 weeks of age, he will only require 6 to 8 relief trips. At the ages of 22 to 32 weeks, the puppy will require about 5 to 7 trips. Adult dogs typically require 4 relief trips per day, in the morning, afternoon, evening and late at night.

You can start out with paper-training indoors and switch over to an outdoor surface as the puppy matures and gains control over his need to eliminate. For the nay-sayers, don't worry—this won't mean that the dog will soil on every piece of newspaper lying around the house. You are training him to go outside, remember? Starting out by paper-training often is the only choice for a city dog.

WHEN YOUR PUPPY'S "GOT TO GO"

Your puppy's need to relieve himself is seemingly non-stop, but signs of improvement will be seen each week. From 8 to 10 weeks old, the puppy will have to be taken outside every time he wakes up, about 10-15 minutes after every meal and after every period of play—all day long, from first thing in the morning until his bedtime! That's a total of ten or more trips per day to teach the puppy where it's okay to relieve himself. With that schedule in mind, you can see that house-training a young puppy is not a part-time job. It requires someone to be home all day.

If that seems overwhelming or impossible, do a little planning. For example, plan to pick up your puppy at the start of a vacation period. If you can't get home in the middle of the day, plan to hire a dog-sitter or ask a neighbor to come over to take the pup outside, feed him his lunch and then take him out again about ten or so minutes after he's eaten. Also make arrangments with that or another person to be your "emergency" contact if you have to stay late on the job. Remind yourself—repeatedly—that this hectic schedule improves as the puppy gets older.

Once you've led your pup to his "bathroom" site a few times, you can let him out to find it on his own, provided you have a securely fenced yard.

CANINE DEVELOPMENT SCHEDULE

It is important to understand how and at what age a puppy develops into adulthood. If you are a puppy owner, consult the following Canine Development Schedule to determine the stage of development your puppy is currently experiencing. This knowledge will help you as you work with the puppy in the weeks and months ahead.

PERIOD	AGE	CHARACTERISTICS
FIRST TO THIRD	BIRTH TO SEVEN WEEKS	Puppy needs food, sleep and warmth and responds to simple and gentle touching. Needs mother for security and disciplining. Needs littermates for learning and interacting with other dogs. Pup learns to function within a pack and learns pack order of dominance. Begin socializing pup with adults and children for short periods. Pup begins to become aware of his environment.
FOURTH	EIGHT TO TWELVE WEEKS	Brain is fully developed. Pup needs socializing with outside world. Remove from mother and littermates. Needs to change from canine pack to human pack. Human dominance necessary. Fear period occurs between 8 and 12 weeks. Avoid fright and pain.
FIFTH	THIRTEEN TO SIXTEEN WEEKS	Training and formal obedience should begin. Less association with other dogs, more with people, places, situations. Period will pass easily if you remember this is pup's change-to-adolescence time. Be firm and fair. Flight instinct prominent. Permissiveness and over-disciplining can do permanent damage. Praise for good behavior.
JUVENILE	FOUR TO EIGHT MONTHS	Another fear period about 7 to 8 months of age. It passes quickly, but be cautious of fright and pain. Sexual maturity reached. Dominant traits established. Dog should understand sit, down, come and stay by now.

NOTE: THESE ARE APPROXIMATE TIME FRAMES. ALLOW FOR INDIVIDUAL DIFFERENCES IN PUPPIES.

The Basset Fauve has a strong nose and he will use it to find a pleasing relief spot. This is the first type of training you will do with your puppy, resulting in a clean adult with good toileting habits.

HOME WITHIN A HOME

Your puppy needs to be confined to one secure, puppy-proof area when no one is able to watch his every move. Generally the kitchen is the place of choice because the floor is washable. Likewise, it's a busy family area that will accustom the pup to a variety of noises, everything from pots and pans to the telephone, blender and dishwasher. He will also be enchanted by the smell of your cooking (and will never be critical when you burn something). An exercise pen (also called an "ex-pen," a puppy version of a playpen) within the room of choice is an excellent means of confinement for a young pup. He can see out and has a certain amount of space in which to run about, but he is safe from dangerous things like electrical cords, heating units, trash baskets or open kitchen-supply cabinets. Place the pen where the puppy

will not get a blast of heat or air conditioning.

In the pen you can put a few toys, his bed (which can be his crate if the dimensions of pen and crate are compatible) and a few layers of newspaper in one small corner, just in case. A water bowl can be hung at a convenient height on the side of the ex-pen so it won't become a splashing pool for an innovative puppy. His food dish can go on the floor, since he's less likely to splash in it.

Crates are something that pet owners are at last getting used to for their dogs. Wild or domestic canines have always preferred to sleep in den-like safe spots, and that is exactly what the crate provides. How often have you

TIDY BOY

Clean by nature, dogs do not like to soil their dens, which in effect are their crates or sleeping quarters. Unless not feeling well, dogs will not defecate or urinate in their crates. Crate training capitalizes on the dog's natural desire to keep his den clean. Be conscientious about giving the puppy as many opportunities to relieve himself outdoors as possible. Reward the puppy for correct behavior. Praise him and pat his head whenever he "goes" in the correct location. Even the tidiest of puppies can have potty accidents, so be patient and dedicate more energy to helping your puppy achieve a clean lifestyle.

seen adult dogs that choose to sleep under a table or chair even though they have full run of the house? It's the den connection.

The crate can be solid (fiberglass) with ventilation on the upper sides and a wire-grate door that locks securely, or it can be of open wire construction with a solid floor. Your puppy will go along with whichever one you prefer. The open wire crate, however, should be covered at night to give the snug feeling of a den. A blanket or towel over the top will be fine.

The crate should be big enough for the adult dog to stand up and turn around in, even though he may spend much of his time curled up in the back part of it. There are movable barriers that fit inside dog crates to provide the right amount of space for small puppies that grow into large dogs. Never afford a young puppy too much space, thinking that you're being kind and generous. He'll just sleep at one end of the crate and soil in the other end! While you should purchase only one crate, one that will accommodate your pup when grown, you will need to make use of the partitions so that the pup has a comfortable area without enough extra space to use as a toilet. A dog does not like to soil where he sleeps, so you are teaching him to "hold it" until it's time for a trip outside. You may want an extra crate to keep in the car for safe traveling.

In your "happy" voice, use the word "Crate" every time you put the pup in his den. If he's new to a crate, toss in a small biscuit for him to chase the first few times.

If you do not have a fenced-in yard, your dog will need to go for walks on leash for potty trips at the scheduled times.

At night, after he's been outside, he should sleep in his crate. The crate may be kept in his designated area at night or, if you want to be sure to hear those wake-up yips in the morning, put the crate in a corner of your bedroom. However, don't make any response whatsoever to whining or crying. If he's completely ignored, he'll settle down and get to sleep.

Good bedding for a young puppy is an old folded bath towel or an old blanket, something that is easily washable and disposable

THE SUCCESS METHOD

Success that comes by luck is usually short-lived. Success that comes by well-thought-out proven methods is often more easily achieved and permanent. This is the Success Method. It is designed to give you, the puppy owner, a simple yet proven way to help your puppy develop clean living habits and a feeling of security in his new environment.

6 STEPS TO SUCCESSFUL CRATE TRAINING

1 Tell the puppy "Crate time!" and place him into the crate with a small treat (a piece of cheese or half of a biscuit). Let him stay in the crate for five minutes while you are in the same room. Then release him and praise lavishly. Never release him when he is fussing. Wait until he is quiet before you let him out.

2 Repeat Step 1 several times a day.

3 The next day, place the puppy into the crate as before. Let him stay there for ten minutes. Do this several times.

4 Continue building time in five-minute increments until the puppy stays in his crate for 30 minutes with you in the room. Always take him to his relief area after prolonged periods in his crate.

5 Now go back to Step 1 and let the puppy stay in his crate for five minutes, this time while you are out of the room.

6 Once again, build crate time in five-minute increments with you out of the room. When the puppy will stay willingly in his crate (he may even fall asleep!) for 30 minutes with you out of the room, he will be ready to stay in it for several hours at a time.

if necessary ("accidents" will happen!). Never put newspaper in the puppy's crate. Those old ideas of adding a clock to replace his mother's heartbeat, or a hot-water bottle to replace her warmth, are just that—old ideas. The clock could drive the puppy nuts, and the hot-water bottle could end up as a very soggy waterbed! An extremely good breeder would have introduced your puppy to the crate by letting two pups sleep together for a couple of nights, followed by several nights alone. How thankful you will be if you found that breeder!

Safe toys in the pup's crate or area will keep him occupied, but monitor their condition closely. Discard any toys that show signs of being chewed to bits. Squeaky

parts, bits of stuffing or plastic or any other small pieces can cause intestinal blockage or possibly choking if swallowed.

PROGRESSING WITH POTTY-TRAINING

After you've taken your puppy out and he has relieved himself in the area you've selected, he can have some free time with the family as long as there is someone responsible for watching him. That doesn't mean just someone in the same room who is watching TV or busy on the computer, but one person who is doing nothing other than keeping an eye on the pup, playing with him on the floor and helping him understand his position in the pack.

This first taste of freedom will let you begin to set the house rules. If you don't want the dog on

If using newspaper as a training aid, it's best to put it near the door that leads outside to his relief area. That way, he will associate that exit with "potty time" and there also will be absorbent material by the door in case he doesn't quite make it outdoors.

SMILE WHEN YOU ORDER ME AROUND!

While trainers recommend practicing with your dog every day, it's perfectly acceptable to take a "mental health day" off. It's better not to train the dog on days when you're in a sour mood. Your bad attitude or lack of interest will be sensed by your dog, and he will respond accordingly. Studies show that dogs are well tuned in to their humans' emotions. Be conscious of how you use your voice when talking to your dog. Raising your voice or shouting will only erode your dog's trust in you as his trainer and master.

BE UPSTANDING!

You are the dog's leader. During training, stand up straight so your dog looks up at you, and therefore up to you. Say the command words clearly, in a clear, declarative tone of voice. (No barking!) Reward as the correct response takes place (remember your timing!). Praise, smiles and treats are "rewards," used to positively reinforce correct responses. Don't repeat a mistake. Just change to another exercise...you will soon find success!

the furniture, now is the time to prevent his first attempts to jump up on the couch. The word to use in this case is "Off," not "Down." "Down" is the word you will use to teach the down position, which is something entirely different.

Most corrections at this stage come in the form of simply distracting the puppy. Instead of telling him "No" for "Don't chew the carpet," distract the chomping puppy with a toy and he'll forget about the carpet.

As you are playing with the pup, do not forget to watch him closely and pay attention to his body language. Whenever you see him begin to circle or sniff, take the puppy outside to relieve himself. If you are paper-training, put him back in his confined area on the newspapers. In either case, praise him as he eliminates, while he actually is in the act of relieving himself. Three seconds after he has finished is too late! You'll be praising him for running toward you, or picking up a toy or whatever he may be doing at that moment, and that's not what you want to be praising him for. Timing is a vital tool in all dog training. Use it!

Remove soiled newspapers immediately and replace them with clean ones. You may want to take a small piece of soiled paper and place it in the middle of the new clean papers, as the scent will attract him to that spot when it's time to go again. That scent attraction is why it's so important to clean up any messes made in the house with a product specially made to eliminate the odor of dog urine and droppings. Regular household cleansers won't do the trick. Pet shops sell the best pet deodorizers. Invest in the largest container you can find.

Scent attraction eventually will lead your pup to his chosen spot outdoors; this is the basis of outdoor training. When you take your puppy outside to relieve himself, use a one-word command such as "Outside" or "Go-potty" (that's one word to the puppy!) as

A favorite of all male dogs is a nice tree on which to leave their calling card.

you pick him up and attach his leash. Then put him down in his area. If for any reason you can't carry him, snap the leash on quickly and lead him to his spot. Now comes the hard part—hard for you, that is. Just stand there until he urinates and defecates. Move him a few feet in one direction or another if he's just sitting there looking at you, but remember that this is neither playtime nor time for a walk. This is strictly a business trip! Then, as he circles and squats (remember your timing!), give him a quiet "Good dog" as praise. If you start to jump for joy, ecstatic over his performance, he'll do one of two things: he will either stop mid-stream, as it were, or he'll do it again for you—in the house—and expect you to be just as delighted!

Give him five minutes or so and, if he doesn't go in that time, take him back indoors to his confined area and try again in

TIME TO PLAY!

Playtime can happen both indoors and out. A young puppy is growing so rapidly that he needs sleep more than he needs a lot of physical exercise. Puppies get sufficient exercise on their own just through normal puppy activity. Monitor play with young children so you can remove the puppy when he's had enough or calm the kids if they get too rowdy. Almost all puppies love to chase after a toy you've thrown, and you can turn your games into educational activities. Every time your puppy brings the toy back to you, say "Give it" (or "Drop it") followed by "Good dog" and throw it again. If he's reluctant to give it to you, offer a small treat so that he drops the toy as he takes the treat. He will soon get the idea!

LEASH TRAINING

House-training and leash training go hand in hand, literally. When taking your puppy outside to do his business, lead him there on his leash. Unless an emergency potty run is called for, do not whisk the puppy up in your arms and take him outside. If you have a fenced yard, you have the advantage of letting the puppy loose to go out, but it's better to put the dog on the leash and take him to his designated place in the yard until he is reliably house-trained. Taking the puppy for a walk is the best way to house-train a dog. The dog will associate the walk with his time to relieve himself, and the exercise of walking stimulates the dog's bowels and bladder. Dogs that are not trained to relieve themselves on a walk may hold it until they get back home, which of course defeats half the purpose of the walk.

another ten minutes, or immediately if you see him sniffing and circling. By careful observation, you'll soon work out a successful schedule.

Accidents, by the way, are just that—accidents. Clean them up quickly and thoroughly, without comment, after the puppy has been taken outside to finish his business and then put back in his area or crate. If you witness an accident in progress, say "No!" in a stern voice and get the pup outdoors immediately. No punishment is needed. You and your puppy are just learning each other's language, and sometimes it's easy to miss a puppy's message. Chalk it up to experience and watch more closely from now on.

KEEPING THE PACK ORDERLY

Discipline is a form of training that brings order to life. For example, military discipline is what allows the soldiers in an army to work as one. Discipline is a form of teaching and, in dogs, is the basis of how the successful pack operates. Each member knows his place in the pack and all respect the leader, or Alpha dog. It is essential for your puppy that you establish this type of relationship, with you as the Alpha, or leader. It is a form of social coexistence that all canines recognize and accept. Discipline, therefore, is never to be confused with punishment. When you teach your puppy how you want him to behave, and he behaves properly and you praise him for it, you are disciplining him with a form of positive reinforcement.

For a dog, rewards come in the form of praise, a smile, a cheerful tone of voice, a few friendly pats or a rub of the ears. Rewards are also small food treats. Obviously, that does not mean bits of regular dog food. Rather, treats are very small bits of special things like cheese or pieces of soft dog treats. The idea is to reward the dog with something very small that he can taste and swallow, providing instant positive reinforcement. If he has to take time to chew the treat, by the time he is finished he will have forgotten what he did to earn it!

Your puppy should never be physically punished. The displeasure shown on your face and in your voice is sufficient to signal to the pup that he has done something wrong. He wants to please everyone higher up on the social ladder, especially his leader, so a scowl and harsh voice will take care of the error. Growling out the word "Shame!" when the pup is caught in the act of doing something wrong is better than the repetitive "No." Some dogs hear "No" so often that they begin to think it's their name! By the way, do not use the dog's name when

KIDS RULE
Children of 10 to 12 year of age are old enough to understand the "be kind to dumb animals" approach and will have fun training their dogs, especially to do tricks. It teaches them to be tolerant, patient and appreciative as well as to accept failure to some extent. Young children can be tyrants, making unreasonable demands of the dog and unable to cope with defeat, blaming it all on the dog. Toddlers need not apply.

you're correcting him. His name is reserved to get his attention for something pleasant about to take place.

There are punishments that have nothing to do with you. For example, your dog may think that chasing cats is one reason for his existence. You can try to stop it as

This is how a dog should look during training—up at his owner, focused on the lesson.

which is a double loop that tightens slightly around the neck, or the head collar, which is similar to a horse's halter. Do not use a chain choke collar unless you have been specifically shown how to put it on and how to use it. If used incorrectly, a chain choke can damage the Basset Fauve's coat.

A lightweight 6-foot woven cotton or nylon training leash is preferred by most trainers because it is easy to fold up in your hand and comfortable to hold because there is a certain amount of give to it. There are lessons where the dog will start off six feet away from you at the end of the leash. The leash used to take the puppy outside to relieve himself is shorter because you don't want him to roam away from his area. The shorter leash will also be the one to use when you walk the puppy, and for the same reason.

much as you like without success, because it's such fun for the dog. But one good hissing, spitting, swipe of a cat's claws across the dog's nose will put an end to the game forever. Only intervene when your dog's eyeball is seriously at risk. Cat scratches can cause permanent damage to an innocent but annoying puppy.

PUPPY KINDERGARTEN

COLLAR AND LEASH

Before you begin your puppy's education, he must be used to his collar and leash. Choose a collar for your puppy that is secure, but not heavy or bulky. He won't enjoy training if he's uncomfortable. A flat buckle collar is fine for everyday wear and for initial puppy training. For older dogs, there are several types of training collars such as the martingale,

Reward your dog with happy breaks for fun time with his toys and with you, his favorite playmate.

A gentle push on the rump will guide your dog into the sit position to show him what you expect when you issue the command.

If you've been fortunate enough to enroll in a Puppy Kindergarten, suggestions will be made as to the best collar and leash for your young puppy. It's "fortunate" because your puppy will be in a class with puppies in his age range (up to five months old) of all breeds and sizes. It's the perfect way for him to learn the right way (and the wrong way) to interact with other dogs as well as their people. You cannot teach your puppy how to interpret another dog's sign language. For a first-time puppy owner, these socialization classes are invaluable. For experienced dog owners, they are a real boon to further training.

ATTENTION

You've been using the dog's name since the minute you collected him from the breeder, so you should be able to get his attention by saying his name—with a big smile and in an excited tone of voice. His response will be the puppy equivalent of "Here I am! What are we going to do?" Your immediate response (if you haven't guessed by now) is "Good dog." Rewarding him at the moment he pays attention to you teaches him the proper way to respond when he hears his name.

EXERCISES FOR A BASIC CANINE EDUCATION

THE SIT EXERCISE

There are several ways to teach the puppy to sit. The first one is to catch him whenever he is about to sit and, as his backside nears the floor, say "Sit, good dog!"

OKAY!

This is the signal that tells your dog that he can quit whatever he was doing. Use "Okay" to end a session on a correct response to a command. (Never end on an incorrect response.) Lots of praise follows. People use "Okay" a lot and it has other uses for dogs, too. Your dog is barking. You say, "Okay! Come!" "Okay" signals him to stop the barking activity and "Come" allows him to come to you for a "Good dog."

That's positive reinforcement and, if your timing is sharp, he will learn that what he's doing at that second is connected to your saying "Sit" and that you think he's clever for doing it!

Another method is to start with the puppy on his leash in front of you. Show him a treat in the palm of your right hand. Bring your hand up under his nose and, almost in slow motion, move your hand up and back so his nose goes up in the air and his head tilts back as he follows the treat in your hand. At that point, he will have to either sit or fall over, so as his back legs buckle under, say "Sit, good dog," and then give him the treat and lots of praise. You may have to begin with your hand lightly running up his chest, actually lifting his chin up until he sits. Some (usually older) dogs require gentle pressure on their hindquarters with the left hand, in which case the dog should be on your left side. Puppies generally do not appreciate this physical dominance.

After a few times, you should be able to show the dog a treat in the open palm of your hand, raise your hand waist-high as you say "Sit" and have him sit. Once again, you have taught him two things at the same time. The verbal command and the motion of the hand are both signals for the sit. Your puppy is watching you almost more than he is

DOWN

"Down" is a harsh-sounding word and a submissive posture in dog body language, thus presenting two obstacles in teaching the down command. When the dog is about to flop down on his own, tell him "Good down." Pups that are not good about being handled learn better by lowering food in front of them. A dog that trusts you can be gently guided into position. When you give the command "Down," be sure to say it sweetly!

listening to you, so what you do is just as important as what you say.

Don't save any of these drills only for training sessions. Use them as much as possible at odd times during a normal day. The dog should always sit before being given his food dish. He should sit to let you go through a doorway first, when the doorbell rings or when you stop to speak to someone on the street.

Once your Basset Fauve has learned the down exercise, you can progress to the down/stay, using your hand signal along with the verbal command.

end of the pup's nose and steadily move your hand down and forward along the ground. Hold the leash to prevent a sudden lunge for the food. As the puppy goes into the down position, say "Down" very gently.

The difficulty with this exercise is twofold: it's both the submissive aspect and the fact that most people say the word "Down" as if they were a drill sergeant in charge of recruits! So issue the command sweetly, give him the treat and have the pup maintain the down position for several seconds. If he tries to get up immediately, place your hands on his shoulders and press down gently, giving him a very quiet "Good dog." As you progress with this lesson, increase the "down time" until he will hold it until you say "Okay" (his cue for release). Practice this one in the house at various times throughout the day.

THE DOWN EXERCISE

Before beginning to teach the down command, you must consider how the dog feels about this exercise. To him, "down" is a submissive position. Being flat on the floor with you standing over him is not his idea of fun. It's up to you to let him know that, while it may not be fun, the reward of your approval is worth his effort.

Start with the puppy on your left side in a sit position. Hold the leash right above his collar in your left hand. Have an extra-special treat, such as a small piece of cooked chicken or hot dog, in your right hand. Place it at the

---

KEEP IT SIMPLE—AND FUN

Practicing obedience is not a military drill. Keep your lessons simple, interesting and user-friendly. Fun breaks help you both. Spend two minutes or ten teaching your puppy, but only practice as long as your dog enjoys what he's doing and is focused on pleasing you. If he's bored or distracted, stop the training session after any correct response (always end on a high note!). After a few minutes of playtime, you can go back to "hitting the books."

By increasing the length of time during which the dog must maintain the down position, you'll find many uses for it. For example, he can lie at your feet in the vet's office or anywhere that both of you have to wait, when you are on the phone, while the family is eating and so forth. If you progress to training for competitive obedience, he'll already be all set for the exercise called the "long down."

THE STAY EXERCISE

To teach the sit/stay, have the dog sit on your left side. Hold the leash at waist level in your left hand and let the dog know that you have a treat in your closed right hand. Step forward on your right foot as you say "Stay." Immediately turn and stand directly in front of the dog, keeping your right hand up high so he'll keep his eye on the treat hand and maintain the sit position for a count of five. Return to your original position and offer the reward.

Increase the length of the sit/stay each time until the dog can hold it for at least 30 seconds without moving. After about a week of success, move out on your right foot and take two steps before turning to face the dog. Give the "Stay" hand signal (left palm back toward the dog's head) as you leave. He gets the treat when you return and he holds the sit/stay. Increase the distance that you walk away from him before turning until you reach the length of your training leash. But don't rush it! Go back to the beginning if he moves before he should. No matter what the lesson, never be upset by having to back up for a few days. The repetition and practice are what will make your

COME AND GET IT!

The come command is your dog's safety signal. Until he is 99% perfect in responding, don't use the come command if you cannot enforce it. Practice on leash with treats or squeakers, or whenever the dog is running to you. Never call him to come to you if he is to be corrected for a misdemeanor. Reward the dog with a treat and happy praise whenever he comes to you.

LET'S GO!

Many people use "Let's go" instead of "Heel" when teaching their dogs to behave on lead. It sounds like more fun! When beginning to teach the heel, whatever command you use, always step off on your left foot. That's the one next to the dog, who is on your left side, in case you've forgotten. Keep a loose leash. When the dog pulls ahead, stop, bring him back and begin again. Use treats to guide him around turns.

dog reliable in these commands. It won't do any good to move on to something more difficult if the command is not mastered at the easier levels. Above all, even if you do get frustrated, never let your puppy know! Always keep a positive, upbeat attitude during training, which will transmit to your dog for positive results!

The down/stay is taught in the same way once the dog is completely reliable and steady with the down command. Again, don't rush it. With the dog in the down position on your left side, step out on your right foot as you say "Stay." Return by walking around in back of the dog and into your original position. While you are training, it's okay to murmur something like "Hold on" to encourage him to stay put. When the dog will stay without moving when you are at a distance of 3 or 4 feet, begin to increase the length of time before you return. Be sure he holds the down on your return until you say "Okay." At that point, he gets his treat—just so he'll remember for next time that it's not over until it's over.

THE COME EXERCISE
No command is more important to the safety of your dog than "come." It is what you should say every single time you see the puppy running toward you: "Binky, come! Good dog." During playtime, run a few feet away from the puppy, turn and tell him to "Come" as he is already running to you. You can go so far as to teach your puppy two things at once if you squat down and hold out your arms. As the pup gets close to you and you're saying "Good dog," bring your right arm in about waist-high.

Now he's also learning the hand signal, an excellent device should you be on the phone when you need to get him to come to you. You'll also both be one step ahead when you enter obedience classes.

Puppies, like children, have notoriously short attention spans, so don't overdo it with any of the training. Keep each lesson short. Break it up with a quick run around the yard or a ball toss, repeat the lesson and quit as soon as the pup gets it right. That way, you will always end with a "Good dog."

When the puppy responds to your well-timed "Come," try it with the puppy on the training leash. This time, catch him off guard, while he's sniffing a leaf or watching a bird: "Binky, come!" You may have to pause for a split second after his name to be sure you have his attention. If the

I WILL FOLLOW YOU

Obedience isn't just a classroom activity. In your home, you have many great opportunities to teach your dog polite manners. Allowing your pet on the bed or furniture elevates him to your level, which is not a good idea (the word is "Off!"). Use the "umbilical cord" method, keeping your dog on lead so he has to go with you wherever you go. You sit, he sits. You walk, he heels. You stop, he sit-stays. Everywhere you go, he's with you, but you go first!

puppy shows any sign of confusion, give the leash a mild jerk and take a couple of steps backward. Do not repeat the command. In this case, as he reaches you, you should say "Good come!"

That's the number-one rule of training. Each command word is given just once. Anything more is nagging. You'll also notice that all commands are one word only. Even when they are actually two words, you say them as one.

Never call the dog to come to you—with or without his name—

A food reward is a surefire way to get your dog to perform his commands, but you will wean him off constant food rewards and focus more on praise and petting for a job done correctly.

FROM HEEL TO ETERNITY
To begin, step away from the dog, who is in the sit position, on your right foot. That tells the dog you aren't going anywhere. Turn and stand directly in front of him so he won't be tempted to follow. Two seconds is a long, long time to your dog, so only increase the time for which he's expected to stay in short increments. Don't force it. When practicing the heel exercise, your dog will sit at your side whenever you stop. Don't stop for more than three seconds, as your enthusiastic dog will really feel like it's an eternity!

if you are angry or intend to correct him for some misbehavior. When correcting the pup, you go to him. Your dog must always connect "come" with something pleasant and with your approval; then you can rely on his response. Life isn't perfect and neither are puppies. A time will come, often around 10 months of age, when he'll become "selectively deaf" or choose to "forget" his name. He may respond by wagging his tail (and even seeming to smile at you) with a look that says "Make me!" Laugh, throw his favorite toy and skip the lesson you had planned. Pups will be pups!

THE HEEL EXERCISE

The second most important command to teach, after the come, is the heel. When you are walking your growing puppy, you need to be in control. Besides, it looks terrible to be pulled and yanked down the street, and it's not much fun either! Your eight-to ten-week old puppy will probably follow you everywhere, but that's his natural instinct, not your control over the situation. However, any time he does follow you, you can say "Heel" and be ahead of the game, as he will learn to associate this command with the action of following you before you even begin teaching him to heel.

There is a very precise, almost military, procedure for teaching your dog to heel. As with other obedience training, begin with the dog on your left side. He will be in a very nice sit and you will have the training leash across your chest. Hold the loop and folded leash in your right hand. Pick up the slack leash above the dog in your left hand and hold it loosely at your side. Step out on your left foot as you say "Heel." If the puppy does not move, give a gentle tug or pat your left leg to get him started. If he surges ahead of you, stop and pull him back gently until he is at your side. Tell him to sit and begin again.

Walk a few steps and stop while the puppy is correctly beside you. Tell him to sit and give mild verbal praise. (More enthusiastic praise will encourage him to think the lesson is over.) Repeat the lesson, only increasing the number of steps you take as long as the dog is heeling nicely beside you. When you end the lesson, have him hold the sit, then give him the "Okay" to let him know that this is the end of the lesson. Praise him so that he knows he did a good job.

The cure for excessive pulling (a common problem) is to stop when the dog is no more than 2 or 3 feet ahead of you. Guide him back into position and begin again. With a really determined puller, try switching to a head collar. This will automatically turn the pup's head toward you so you can bring him back easily to the heel position. Give quiet, reassuring praise every time the leash goes slack and he's staying with you.

Staying and heeling can take a lot out of a dog, so provide playtime and free-running exercise when the lessons are over to shake off the stress. You don't want him to associate training with all work and no fun.

TAPERING OFF TIDBITS

Your dog has been watching you—and the hand that treats—throughout all of his lessons, and now it's time to break the treat habit. Begin by giving him treats at the end of each lesson only. Then start to give a treat after the end of only some of the lessons. At the end of every lesson, as well as during the lessons, be consistent with the praise. Your pup

now doesn't know if he'll get a treat or not, but he should keep performing well just in case! Finally, you will stop giving treat rewards entirely. Save them for something brand-new that you want to teach him. Keep up the praise and you'll always have a "good dog."

Training brings out the true potential in your Basset Fauve, a breed that makes delightful students.

SHOULD WE ENROLL?

If you have the means and the time, you should definitely take your dog to obedience classes. Begin with Kindergarten Puppy Classes in which puppies of all sizes learn basic lessons while getting the opportunity to meet and greet each other; it's as much about socialization as it is about good manners. What you learn in class you can practice at home. And if you goof up in practice, you'll get help in the next session.

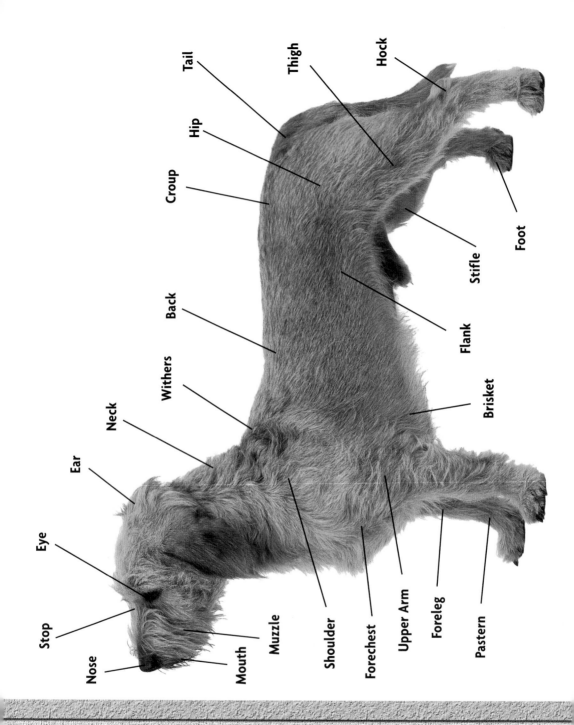

Tail

Thigh

Hock

Hip

Croup

Back

Withers

Neck

Ear

Eye

Stop

Nose

Mouth

Muzzle

Shoulder

Forechest

Upper Arm

Foreleg

Pastern

Brisket

Flank

Stifle

Foot

PHYSICAL STRUCTURE OF THE BASSET FAUVE DE BRETAGNE

BASSET FAUVE DE BRETAGNE

By Lowell Ackerman DVM, DACVD

HEALTHCARE FOR A LIFETIME

When you own a dog, you become his healthcare advocate over his entire lifespan, as well as being the one to shoulder the financial burden of such care. Accordingly, it is worthwhile to focus on prevention rather than treatment, as you and your pet will both be happier.

Of course, the best place to have begun your program of preventive healthcare is with the initial purchase or adoption of your dog. There is no way of guaranteeing that your new furry friend is free of medical problems, but there are some things you can do to improve your odds. You certainly should have done adequate research into the Basset Fauve and have located a reputable breeder. Health issues aside, a large number of pet abandonment and relinquishment cases arise from a mismatch between pet needs and owner expectations. This is entirely preventable with appropriate planning and finding a good breeder.

Regarding healthcare issues specifically, it is very difficult to make blanket statements about where to acquire a problem-free pet, but, again, a reputable breeder is your best bet. In an ideal situation you have the opportunity to see both parents, get references from other owners of the breeder's pups and see genetic-testing documentation for several generations of the litter's ancestors. At the very least, you must thoroughly investigate the Basset Fauve and the problems inherent in the breed, as well as the genetic testing available to screen for those problems. Genetic testing offers some important benefits, but testing is available for only a few disorders in a relatively small number of breeds and is not available for some of the most common genetic diseases, such as hip dysplasia, cataracts, epilepsy, cardiomyopathy, etc. This area of research is indeed exciting and increasingly important, and advances will continue to be made each year. In fact, recent research has

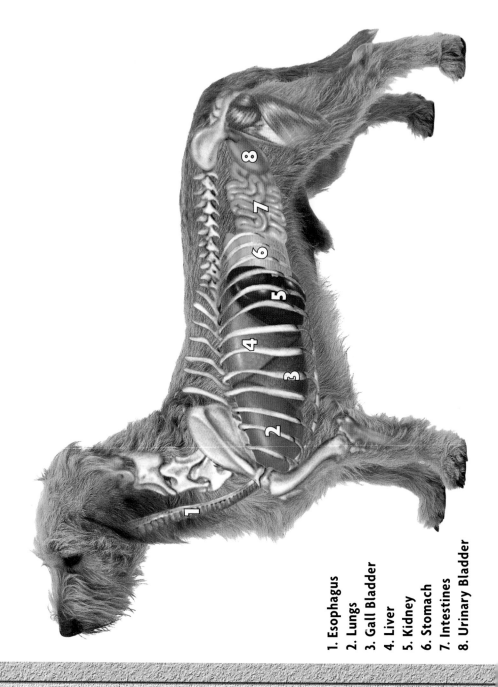

1. Esophagus
2. Lungs
3. Gall Bladder
4. Liver
5. Kidney
6. Stomach
7. Intestines
8. Urinary Bladder

INTERNAL ORGANS OF THE BASSET FAUVE DE BRETAGNE

shown that there is an equivalent dog gene for 75% of known human genes, so research done in either species is likely to benefit the other.

We've also discussed that evaluating the behavioral nature of your Basset Fauve and that of his immediate family members is an important part of the selection process that cannot be underestimated or overemphasized. It is sometimes difficult to evaluate temperament in puppies because certain behavioral tendencies, such as some forms of aggression, may not be immediately evident. More dogs are euthanized each year for behavioral reasons than for all medical conditions combined, so it

DOGGIE DENTAL DON'TS
A veterinary dental exam is necessary if you notice one or any combination of the following in your dog:
• Broken, loose or missing teeth
• Loss of appetite (which could be due to mouth pain or illness caused by infection)
• Gum abnormalities, including redness, swelling and/or bleeding
• Drooling, with or without blood
• Yellowing of the teeth and/or gumline, indicating tartar
• Bad breath.

is critical to take temperament issues seriously. Start with a well-balanced, friendly companion and put the time and effort into proper

Healthy teeth lead to better overall health, as gum disease-causing bacteria can travel through the body to infect the vital organs, causing serious problems.

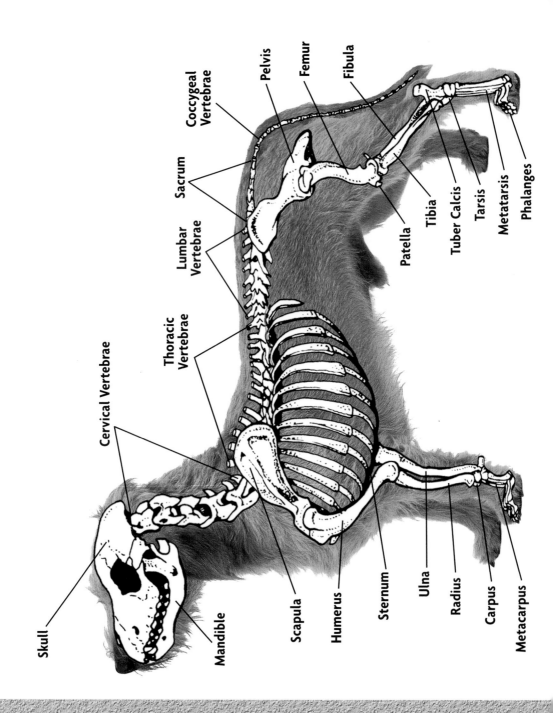

Coccygeal Vertebrae

Pelvis

Femur

Fibula

Sacrum

Tibia

Patella

Tuber Calcis

Tarsis

Metatarsis

Phalanges

Lumbar Vertebrae

Thoracic Vertebrae

Cervical Vertebrae

Skull

Mandible

Scapula

Humerus

Sternum

Ulna

Radius

Carpus

Metacarpus

SKELETAL STRUCTURE OF THE BASSET FAUVE DE BRETAGNE

An outdoor run is an option for a safe area for free play, as long as it's spacious, with access to shelter and shade, and that the dogs are provided with plenty of water.

socialization, and you will both be rewarded with a lifelong valued relationship.

Assuming that you have started off with a pup from healthy, sound stock, you then become responsible for helping your veterinarian keep your pet healthy. Some crucial things happen before you even bring your puppy home. Parasite control typically begins at two weeks of age, and vaccinations typically begin at six to eight weeks of age. A pre-pubertal evaluation is typically scheduled for about six months of age. At this time, a dental evaluation is done (since the adult teeth are now in), heartworm prevention is started and neutering or spaying is most commonly done.

It is critical to commence regular dental care at home if you have not already done so. It may not sound very important, but most dogs have active periodontal disease by four years of age if they don't have their teeth cleaned regularly at home, not just at their veterinary exams. Dental problems lead to more than just bad "doggie breath": gum disease can have very serious medical consequences. If you start brushing your dog's teeth and using antiseptic rinses from a young age, your dog will be accustomed to it and will not resist. The results will be healthy dentition, which your pet will need to enjoy a long, healthy life.

Most dogs are considered adults at a year of age, although

When your Basset Fauve reaches three-quarters of his anticipated lifespan, he is considered a "senior" and likely requires some special care. In general, if you've been taking great care of your canine companion throughout his formative and adult years, the transition to senior status should be a smooth one. Age is not a disease, and as long as everything is functioning as it should, there is no reason why most of late adulthood should not be rewarding for both you and your Basset Fauve. This is especially true if you have tended to the details, such as regular veterinary visits, proper dental care, excellent nutrition and management of bone and joint issues.

There could be unseen dangers lurking in the tall grass, such as chemicals and fertilizers, insects, allergens and other irritants. Check your dog's skin and coat regularly, especially after time outdoors.

some larger breeds still have some filling out to do up to about two or so years old. Even individual dogs within each breed have different healthcare requirements, so work with your veterinarian to determine what will be needed and what your role should be. This doctor-client relationship is important, because as vaccination guidelines change, there may not be an annual "vaccine visit" scheduled. You must make sure that you see your veterinarian at least annually, even if no vaccines are due, because this is the best opportunity to coordinate healthcare activities and to make sure that no medical issues creep by unaddressed.

PROBLEM: AND THAT STARTS WITH "P"

Urinary tract problems more commonly affect female dogs, especially those who have been spayed. The first sign that a urinary tract problem exists is usually a strong odor from the urine or an unusual color. Blood in the urine, known as hematuria, is another sign of an infection, related to cystitis, a bladder infection, bladder cancer or a blood-clotting disorder. Urinary tract problems can also be signaled by the dog's straining while urinating, experiencing pain during urination and genital discharge as well as excessive water intake and urination.

THE ABCs OF
Emergency Care

Abrasions
Clean wound with running water or 3% hydrogen peroxide. Pat dry with gauze and spray with antibiotic. Do not cover.

Animal Bites
Clean area with soap and saline or water. Apply pressure to any bleeding area. Apply antibiotic ointment.

Antifreeze Poisoning
Induce vomiting and take dog to the vet.

Bee Sting
Remove stinger and apply soothing lotion or cold compress; give antihistamine in proper dosage.

Bleeding
Apply pressure directly to wound with gauze or towel for five to ten minutes. If wound does not stop bleeding, wrap wound with gauze and adhesive tape.

Bloat/Gastric Torsion
Immediately take the dog to the vet or emergency clinic; phone from car. No time to waste.

Burns
Chemical: Bathe dog with water and pet shampoo. Rinse in saline. Apply antibiotic ointment.

Acid: Rinse with water. Apply one part baking soda, two parts water to affected area.

Alkali: Rinse with water. Apply one part vinegar, four parts water to affected area.

Electrical: Apply antibiotic ointment. Seek veterinary assistance immediately.

Choking
If the dog is on the verge of collapsing, wedge a solid object, such as the handle of a screwdriver, between molars on one side of mouth to keep mouth open. Pull tongue out. Use long-nosed pliers or fingers to remove foreign object. Do not push the object down the dog's throat. For small or medium dogs, hold dog upside down by hind legs and shake firmly to dislodge foreign object.

Chlorine Ingestion
With clean water, rinse the mouth and eyes. Give dog water to drink; contact the vet.

Constipation
Feed dog 2 tablespoons bran flakes with each meal. Encourage drinking water. Mix 1/4 teaspoon mineral oil in dog's food.

Diarrhea
Withhold food for 12 to 24 hours. Feed dog anti-diarrheal with eyedropper. When feeding resumes, feed one part boiled hamburger, one part plain cooked rice, 1/4- to 3/4-cup four times daily.

Dog Bite
Snip away hair around puncture wound; clean with 3% hydrogen peroxide; apply tincture of iodine. If wound appears deep, take the dog to the vet.

Frostbite
Wrap the dog in a heavy blanket. Warm affected area with a warm bath for ten minutes. Red color to skin will return with circulation; if tissues are pale after 20 minutes, contact the vet.

Heat Stroke
Submerge the dog in cold water; if no response within ten minutes, contact the vet.

Hot Spots
Mix 2 packets Domeboro® with 2 cups water. Saturate cloth with mixture and apply to hot spots for 15-30 minutes. Apply antibiotic ointment. Repeat every six to eight hours.

Poisonous Plants
Wash affected area with soap and water. Cleanse with alcohol. For foxtail/grass, apply antibiotic ointment.

Rat Poison Ingestion
Induce vomiting. Keep dog calm, maintain dog's normal body temperature (use blanket or heating pad). Get to the vet for antidote.

Shock
Keep the dog calm and warm; call for veterinary assistance.

Snake Bite
If possible, bandage the area and apply pressure. If the area is not conducive to bandaging, use ice to control bleeding. Get immediate help from the vet.

Tick Removal
Apply flea and tick spray directly on tick. Wait one minute. Using tweezers or wearing plastic gloves, grasp the tick's body firmly. Apply antibiotic ointment.

Vomiting
Restrict dog's water intake; offer a few ice cubes. Withhold food for next meal. Contact vet if vomiting persists longer than 24 hours.

At this stage in your Basset Fauve's life, your veterinarian may want to schedule visits twice yearly, instead of once, to run some laboratory screenings, electrocardiograms and the like, and to change the diet to something more digestible. Catching problems early is the best way to manage them effectively. Treating the early stages of heart disease is so much easier than trying to intervene when there is more significant damage to the heart muscle. Similarly, managing the beginning of kidney problems is fairly routine if there is no significant kidney damage. Other problems, like cognitive dysfunction (similar to senility and Alzheimer's disease), cancer, diabetes and arthritis, are more common in older dogs, but all can be treated to help the dog live as many happy, comfortable years as possible. Just as in people, medical management is more effective (and less expensive) when you catch things early.

SELECTING A VETERINARIAN

There is probably no more important decision that you will make regarding your pet's health-care than the selection of his doctor. Your pet's veterinarian will be a pediatrician, family-

SAMPLE VACCINATION SCHEDULE

6-8 weeks of age	Parvovirus, Distemper, Adenovirus-2 (Hepatitis)
9-11 weeks of age	Parvovirus, Distemper, Adenovirus-2 (Hepatitis)
12-14 weeks of age	Parvovirus, Distemper, Adenovirus-2 (Hepatitis)
12-16 weeks of age	Rabies
1 year of age	Parvovirus, Distemper, Adenovirus-2 (Hepatitis), Rabies

Revaccination is performed every one to three years, depending on the product, the method of administration and the patient's risk. Initial adult inoculation (for dogs at least 16 weeks of age in which a puppy series was not done or could not be confirmed) is two vaccinations, done three to four weeks apart, with revaccination according to the same criteria mentioned. Other vaccines are given as decided between owner and veterinarian.

practice physician and gerontologist, depending on the dog's life stage, and will be the individual who makes recommendations regarding issues such as when specialists need to be consulted, when diagnostic testing and/or therapeutic intervention is needed and when you will need to seek outside emergency and critical-care services. Your vet will act as your advocate and liaison throughout these processes.

Everyone has his own idea about what to look for in a vet, an individual who will play a big role in his dog's (and, of course, his own) life for many years to come. For some, it is the compassionate caregiver with whom they hope to develop a professional relationship to span the lifetime of their dogs and even their future pets. For others, they are seeking a clinician with keen diagnostic and therapeutic insight who can deliver state-of-the-art healthcare. Still others need a veterinary facility that is open evenings and weekends, or is in close proximity or provides mobile veterinary services, to accommodate their schedules; these people may not much mind that their dogs might see different veterinarians on each visit. Just as we have different reasons for selecting our own healthcare professionals (e.g., covered by insurance plan, expert in field, convenient location, etc.), we should not expect that there is

a one-size-fits-all recommendation for selecting a veterinarian and veterinary practice. The best advice is to be honest in your assessment of what you expect from a veterinary practice and to conscientiously research the options in your area. You will quickly appreciate that not all veterinary practices are the same, and you will be happiest with one that truly meets your needs.

There is another point to be considered in the selection of veterinary services. Not that long ago, a single veterinarian would attempt to manage all medical and

BEWARE THE SPIDER
Should you worry about a spider spinning her sticky web over your dog? Like other venomous critters, spiders can bite dogs and cause severe reactions. The most deleterious eight-leggers are the black and red widow spiders, brown recluse and common brown spiders, whose bites can cause local pain, cramping, spasms and restlessness. It is these signals that tell owners there is a problem, as the bites themselves can be difficult to locate under your dog's coat. Another vicious arachnid is the bark scorpion, whose bite can cause excessive drooling, tearing, urination and defecation. Often spider and scorpion bites are misdiagnosed because vets don't recognize the signs and owners didn't witness the escape of the avenging arachnid.

HIT ME WITH A HOT SPOT

What is a hot spot? Technically known as pyotraumatic dermatitis, a hot spot is an infection on the dog's coat, usually by the rear end, under the tail or on a leg, which the dog inflicts upon himself. The dog licks and bites the itchy spot until it becomes inflamed and infected. The hot spot can range in size from the circumference of a grape to the circumference of an apple. Provided that the hot spot is not related to a deeper bacterial infection, it can be treated topically by clipping the area, cleaning the sore and giving prednisone. For bacterial infections, antibiotics are required. In some cases, an Elizabethan collar is required to keep the dog from further irritating the hot spot. The itching can intensify and the pain becomes worse. Medicated shampoos and cool compresses, drying agents and topical steroids may be prescribed by your vet as well. Hot spots can be caused by fleas, an allergy, an ear infection, anal sac problems, mange or a foreign irritant. Likewise, they can be linked to psychoses. The underlying problem must be addressed in addition to the hot spot. Generally, dogs with heavier and longer coats are more prone to hot spots than the Basset Fauve.

was just impossible for general veterinary practitioners to be experts in every species, every field and every ailment. However, just as in the human healthcare fields, specialization has allowed general practitioners to concentrate on primary healthcare delivery, especially wellness and the prevention of infectious diseases, and to utilize a network of specialists to assist in the management of conditions that require specific expertise and experience. Thus there are now many types of veterinary specialists, including dermatologists, cardiologists, ophthalmologists, surgeons, internists, oncologists, neurologists, behaviorists, criticalists and others to help primary-care veterinarians deal with complicated medical challenges. In most cases, specialists see cases referred by primary-care veterinarians, make diagnoses and set up management plans. From there, the animals' ongoing care is returned to their primary-care veterinarians. This important team approach to your pet's medical-care needs has provided opportunities for advanced care and an unparalleled level of quality to be delivered.

With all of the opportunities for your Basset Fauve to receive high-quality veterinary medical care, there is another topic that needs to be addressed at the same time—cost. It's been said that you

surgical issues as they arose. That was often problematic, because veterinarians are trained in many species and many diseases, and it can have excellent healthcare or inexpensive healthcare, but never both; this is as true in veterinary medicine as it is in human medicine. While veterinary costs are a fraction of what the same services cost in the human health-care arena, it is still difficult to deal with unanticipated medical costs, especially since they can easily creep into hundreds or even thousands of dollars if specialists or emergency services become involved. However, there are ways of managing these risks. The easiest is to buy pet health insurance and realize that its foremost purpose is not to cover routine healthcare visits but rather to serve as an umbrella for those rainy days when your pet needs medical care and you don't want to worry about whether or not you can afford that care.

Pet insurance policies are very cost-effective (and very inexpensive by human health-insurance standards), but make sure that you buy the policy long before you intend to use it (preferably starting in puppyhood, because coverage will exclude pre-existing conditions) and that you are actually buying an indemnity insurance plan from an insurance company that is regulated by your state or province. Many insurance policy look-alikes are actually discount clubs that are redeemable only at specific locations and for specific services. An

indemnity plan covers your pet at almost all veterinary, specialty and emergency practices and is an excellent way to manage your pet's ongoing healthcare needs.

VACCINATIONS AND INFECTIOUS DISEASES

There has never been an easier time to prevent a variety of infectious diseases in your dog, but the advances we've made in veterinary medicine come with a price—choice. Now while it may seem that choice is a good thing (and it is), it has never been more difficult for the pet owner (or the veterinarian) to make an informed decision about the best way to protect pets through vaccination.

Years ago, it was just accepted that puppies got a starter series of vaccinations and then annual "boosters" throughout their lives to keep them protected. As more and more vaccines became available, consumers wanted the convenience of having all of that protection in a single injection. The result was "multivalent" vaccines that crammed a lot of protection into a single syringe. The manufacturers' recommendations were to give the vaccines annually, and this was a simple enough protocol to follow. However, as veterinary medicine has become more sophisticated and we have started looking more at healthcare quandaries rather than convenience, it became necessary to reevaluate the situation and deal with some tough questions. It is important to realize that whether or not to use a particular vaccine depends on the risk of contracting the disease against which it protects, the severity of the disease if it is contracted, the duration of immunity provided by the vaccine, the safety of the product and the needs of the individual animal. In a very general sense, rabies, distemper, hepatitis and parvovirus are considered core vaccine needs, while parain-fluenza, *Bordetella bronchiseptica*, leptospirosis, coronavirus and borreliosis (Lyme disease) are considered non-core needs and best reserved for animals that demonstrate reasonable risk of contracting the diseases.

THE GREAT VACCINATION DEBATE
What kinds of questions need to be addressed? When the vet injects multiple organisms at the same time, might some of the components interfere with one another in the development of immunologic protection? We don't have the comprehensive answer to that question, but it does appear that the immune system better handles agents when given individually. Unfortunately, most manufacturers still bundle their vaccine components because that is what most pet owners want, so

getting vaccines with single components can sometimes be difficult.

Another question has to do with how often vaccines should be given. Again, this seems to be different for each vaccine component. There seems to be a general consensus that a puppy (or a dog with an unknown vaccination history) should get a series of vaccinations to initially stimulate his immunity and then a booster at one year of age, but even the veterinary associations and colleges have trouble reaching agreement about what he should get after that. Rabies vaccination schedules are not debated, because vaccine schedules for this contagious and devastating disease are determined by govern-ment agencies. Regarding the rest, some recommend that we continue to give the vaccines annually because this method has worked well as a disease preven-tive for decades and delivers predictable protection. Others recommend that some of the vaccines need to be given only every second or third year, as this can be done without affecting levels of protection. This is probably true for some vaccine components (such as hepatitis), but there have been no large studies to demonstrate what the optimal interval should be and whether the same principles hold true for all breeds.

It may be best to just measure titers, which are protective blood levels of various vaccine components, on an annual basis, but that too is not without controversy. Scientists have not precisely determined the minimum titer of specific vaccine components that will be guaranteed to provide a pet with protection. Pets with very high titers will clearly be protected and those with very low titers will need repeat vaccinations, but there is also a large "gray zone" of pets that probably have intermediate protection and may or may not need repeat vaccination, depending on their risk of coming into contact with the disease.

These questions leave primary-care veterinarians in a very uncomfortable position, one that is not easy to resolve. Do they recommend annual vaccination in a manner that has demonstrated successful protection for decades, do they recommend skipping vaccines some years and hope that the protection lasts or do they measure blood tests (titers) and hope that the results are convincing enough to clearly indicate whether repeat vaccination is warranted?

These aren't the only vaccination questions impacting pets, owners and veterinarians. Other controversies focus on whether vaccines should be dosed according to body weight

(currently they are administered in uniform doses, regardless of the animal's size), whether there are breed-specific issues important in determining vaccination programs (for instance, we know that some breeds have a harder time mounting an appropriate immune response to parvovirus vaccine and might benefit from a different dose or injection interval) and which type of vaccine—live-virus or inactivated—offers more advantages with fewer disadvantages. Clearly, there are many more questions than there are answers. The important thing, as a pet owner, is to be aware of the issues and be able to work with your veterinarian to make decisions that are right for your pet. Be an informed consumer and you will appreciate the deliberation required in tailoring a vaccination program to best meet the needs of your pet. Expect also that this is an ongoing, everchanging topic of debate; thus, the

Allergies can make for an itchy dog—and a good roll in the grass sure scratches the itch!

If food allergy is the diagnosis, you will have to try alternative diets until you eliminate the ingredients to which your dog is allergic.

decisions you make this year won't necessarily be the same as the ones you make next year.

COMMON VACCINATIONS

Now that you are more confused than ever about vaccination, it is a good time to discuss some of the diseases that create the need for vaccination in the first place. Following are the major canine infectious diseases and a simple explanation of each.

Rabies is a devastating viral disease that can be fatal in dogs and people. In fact, vaccination of dogs and cats is an important public-health measure to create a resistant animal buffer population to protect people from contracting the disease. Vaccination schedules are determined on a government level and are not optional for pet owners; rabies vaccination is required by law in all 50 states.

Parvovirus is a severe, potentially life-threatening disease that is easily transmitted between dogs. There are four strains of the virus, but it is believed that there is significant "cross-protection" between strains that may be included in individual vaccines.

Distemper is another potentially severe and life-threatening disease with a relatively high risk of exposure, especially in certain regions. In very high-risk distemper environments, young pups may be vaccinated with human measles vaccine, a related virus that offers cross-protection when administered at 4-10 weeks of age.

Hepatitis is caused by canine adenovirus type 1 (CAV-1), but since vaccination with the causative virus has a higher rate of adverse effects, cross-protection is derived from the use of adenovirus type 2 (CAV-2), a cause of respiratory disease and one of the potential causes of canine cough. Vaccination with CAV-2 provides long-term immunity against hepatitis, but relatively less protection against respiratory infection.

Canine cough (tracheobronchitis) is actually a fairly complicated result of viral and bacterial offenders; therefore, even with vaccination, protection is incomplete. Wherever dogs congregate, canine cough will likely be spread among them. Intranasal vaccination with *Bordetella* and parainfluenza is the best safeguard, but the duration of immunity does not appear to be very long, typically a year at most. These are non-core vaccines, but vaccination is sometimes mandated by boarding kennels, obedience classes, dog shows and other places where dogs congregate to try to minimize spread of infection.

Leptospirosis is a potentially fatal disease that is more common in some geographic regions. It is capable of being spread to humans. The disease varies with the individual "serovar," or strain, of Leptospira involved; since there does not appear to be much cross-protection between serovars, protection is only as good as the likelihood that the serovar in the vaccine is the same as the one in the pet's local environment. Problems with Leptospira vaccines are that protection does not last very long, side effects are not uncommon and a large percentage of dogs (perhaps 30%) may not respond to vaccination.

Lyme disease is caused by *Borrelia burgdorferi*; the risk of being infected varies with the geographic area in which the pet lives and travels. Lyme disease is spread by deer ticks in the eastern US and western black-legged ticks

FOOD ALLERGY

Severe itching, leading to bald patches and open sores on the feet, face, ears, armpits and groin, could be caused by a food allergy. Studies indicate that up to 10% of dogs suffer from food allergies, which develop slowly over time without a change in diet. Dogs who suffer from chronic ear problems may actually have a food allergy. Unfortunately, there are no tests available to determine that your dog definitely suffers from a food allergy. The dog will be miserable and you will be frustrated and stressed. Take the problem into your own hands and kitchen. Select a type of meat that your dog is not getting from his existing diet, perhaps white fish, lamb or venison, and prepare a home-cooked food. The food should consist of two parts carbohydrate (rice, pasta or potatoes) and one part protein (the chosen meat). It's better not to start with soy as the protein source, unless all of the meats cause a reaction.

Monitor your dog's intake carefully. He must eat only your prepared meal without any treats or side-trips to the garbage bin. All family members (and visiting friends) must be informed of the plan. After four or five weeks on the new diet, you will reintroduce a portion of his original diet to determine if this food is the cause of the skin irritation (or other reactions). Once the dog reacts to the change in diet, resume the new diet. Make dietary modifications every two weeks and keep careful records of any reactions the dog has to the diet.

in the western part of the country, and the risk of exposure is high in some regions. Lameness, fever and inappetence are most commonly seen in affected dogs. The extent of protection from the vaccine has not been conclusively demonstrated.

Coronavirus has a high risk of exposure, especially in areas where dogs congregate, but it typically causes only mild to moderate digestive upset (diarrhea, vomiting, etc.). Vaccines are available, but the duration of protection is believed to be relatively short and the effectiveness of the vaccine in preventing infection is considered low.

There are many other vaccinations available, including those for *Giardia* and canine adenovirus-1. While there may be some specific indications for their use, and local risk factors to be considered, they are not widely recommended for most dogs.

NEUTERING/SPAYING
Sterilization procedures (neutering for males/spaying for females) are meant to accomplish several purposes. While the underlying premise is to address the risk of pet overpopulation, there are also some medical and behavioral benefits to the surgeries as well. For females, spaying prior to the first estrus (heat cycle) leads to a marked reduction in the risk of mammary cancer. There also will

be no manifestations of "heat" to attract male dogs and no bleeding in the house. For males, there is prevention of testicular cancer and a reduction in the risk of prostate problems. In both sexes there may be some limited reduction in aggressive behaviors toward other dogs, and some diminishing of urine marking, roaming and mounting.

While neutering and spaying do indeed prevent animals from contributing to pet overpopulation, even no-cost and low-cost neutering options have not eliminated the problem. Perhaps one of the main reasons for this is that individuals that intentionally breed their dogs and those that allow their animals to run at large are the main causes of unwanted offspring. Also, animals in shelters are often there because they were abandoned or relinquished, not because they came from unplanned matings. Neutering/spaying is important, but it should be considered in the context of the real causes of animals' ending up in shelters and eventually being euthanized.

One of the important considerations regarding neutering is that it is a surgical procedure. This sometimes gets lost in discussions of low-cost procedures and commoditization of the process. In females, spaying is specifically referred to as an ovariohysterectomy. In this procedure, a midline incision is made in the abdomen and the entire uterus and both ovaries are surgically removed. While this is a major invasive surgical procedure, it usually has few complications, because it is typically performed on healthy young animals. However, it is major surgery, as any woman who has had a hysterectomy will attest.

In males, neutering has traditionally referred to castration, which involves the surgical removal of both testicles. While still a significant piece of surgery, there is not the abdominal exposure that is required in the female surgery. In addition, there is now a chemical sterilization option, in which a solution is injected into each testicle, leading to atrophy of the sperm-producing cells. This can typically be done under sedation rather than full anesthesia. This is a relatively new approach, and there are no long-term clinical studies yet available.

Neutering/spaying is typically done around six months of age at most veterinary hospitals, although techniques have been pioneered to perform the procedures in animals as young as eight weeks of age. In general, the surgeries on the very young animals are done for the specific reason of sterilizing them before they go to their new homes. This is done in some shelter hospitals for assurance that the animals will definitely not produce any pups.

Otherwise, these organizations need to rely on owners to comply with their wishes to have the animals "altered" at a later date, something that does not always happen.

There are some exciting immunocontraceptive "vaccines" currently under development, and there may be a time when contraception in pets will not require surgical procedures. We anxiously await these developments.

Knowing your dog well and performing regular hands-on checks will help you discover any potential health problems early on.

A scanning electron micrograph of a dog flea, Ctenocephalides canis, *on dog hair.*

EXTERNAL PARASITES

FLEAS

Fleas have been around for millions of years and, while we have better tools now for controlling them than at any time in the past, there still is little chance that they will end up on an endangered species list. Actually, they are very well adapted to living on our pets, and they continue to adapt as we make advances.

The female flea can consume 15 times her weight in blood during active reproduction and can lay as many as 40 eggs a day. These eggs are very resistant to the effects of insecticides. They hatch into larvae, which then mature and spin cocoons. The immature fleas reside in this pupal stage until the time is right for feeding. This pupal stage is also very resistant to the effects of insecticides, and pupae can last in the environment without feeding for many months. Newly emergent fleas are attracted to animals by the warmth of the animals' bodies, movement and exhaled carbon dioxide. However, when they first emerge from their cocoons, they orient towards light; thus, when an animal passes between a flea and the light source, casting a shadow, the flea pounces and starts to feed. If the animal turns out to be a dog or cat, the reproductive cycle continues. If the flea lands on another type of animal, including a person, the flea will bite but will then look for a more appropriate host. An emerging adult flea can survive without feeding for up to 12 months but, once it tastes blood, it can only survive off its host for three to four days.

It was once thought that fleas spend most of their lives in the environment, but we now know that fleas won't willingly jump off a dog unless leaping to another dog or when physically removed by brushing, bathing or other manipulation. Flea eggs, on the other hand, are shiny and smooth, and they roll off the animal and into the environment. The eggs, larvae and pupae then exist in the environment, but once the adult finds a susceptible animal, it's home sweet home until the flea is forced to seek refuge elsewhere.

Since adult fleas live on the animal and immature forms survive in the environment, a successful treatment plan must address all stages of the flea life cycle. There are now several safe and effective flea-control products that can be applied on a monthly

> ### FLEA PREVENTION FOR YOUR DOG
> • Discuss with your veterinarian the safest product to protect your dog, likely in the form of a monthly tablet or a liquid preparation placed on the back of the dog's neck.
> • For dogs suffering from flea-bite dermatitis, a shampoo or topical insecticide treatment is required.
> • Your lawn and property should be sprayed with an insecticide   designed to kill fleas and ticks that lurk outdoors.
> • Using a flea comb, check the dog's coat regularly for any signs of parasites.
> • Practice good housekeeping: Vacuum floors, carpets and furniture regularly, especially in the areas that the dog frequents, and wash the dog's bedding weekly.
> • Follow up house-cleaning with carpet shampoos and sprays to rid the house of fleas at all stages of development. Insect growth regulators are the safest option.

basis. These include fipronil, imidacloprid, selamectin and permethrin (found in several formulations). Most of these products have significant flea-killing rates within 24 hours. However, none of them will control the immature forms in the environment. To accomplish this, there are a variety of insect growth regulators that can be

THE FLEA'S LIFE CYCLE

What came first, the flea or the egg? This age-old mystery is more difficult to comprehend than the

actual cycle of the flea. Fleas usually live only about four months. A female can lay 2,000 eggs in her lifetime.

Egg

After ten days of rolling around your carpet or under your furniture, the eggs hatch into larvae,

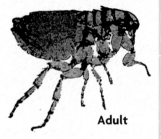

Larva

which feed on various and sundry debris. In days or months, depending on the climate, the larvae spin a cocoon and develop into the pupal or nymph stage, which quickly develop into fleas.

Pupa

These immature fleas must locate a host within 10 to 14 days or they will die. Only about 1% of the flea population exist as adult fleas, while the other 99% exist as eggs, larvae or pupae.

Adult

KILL FLEAS THE NATURAL WAY

If you choose not to go the route of conventional medication, there are some natural ways to ward off fleas:
• Dust your dog with a natural flea powder, composed of such herbal goodies as rosemary, wormwood, pennyroyal, citronella, rue, tobacco powder and eucalyptus.
• Apply diatomaceous earth, the fossilized remains of single-cell algae, to your carpets, furniture and pet's bedding. Even though it's not good for dogs, it's even worse for fleas, which will dry up swiftly and die.
• Brush your dog frequently, give him adequate exercise and let him fast occasionally. All of these activities strengthen the dog's system and make him more resistant to disease and parasites.
• Bathe your dog with a capful of pennyroyal or eucalyptus oil.
• Feed a natural diet, free of additives and preservatives. Add some fresh garlic and brewer's yeast to the dog's morning portion, as these have flea-repelling properties.

sprayed into the environment (e.g., pyriproxyfen, methoprene, fenoxycarb) as well as insect development inhibitors such as lufenuron that can be administered. These compounds have no effect on adult fleas, but they stop immature forms from developing into adults. In years gone by we relied heavily on toxic insecticides (such as organophosphates, organochlorines and carbamates) to manage the flea problem, but today's options are not only much safer to use on our pets but also safer for the environment.

TICKS

Ticks are members of the spider class (arachnids) and are blood-sucking parasites capable of transmitting a variety of diseases, including Lyme disease, ehrlichiosis, babesiosis and Rocky Mountain spotted fever. It's easy to see ticks on your own skin, but it is more of a challenge when your Basset Fauve is affected. Whenever you happen to be planning a stroll in a tick-infested area (especially forests, grassy or wooded areas or parks) be prepared to do a thorough inspection of your dog afterward to search for ticks. Ticks can be tricky, so make sure you spend time looking in the ears, between the toes and everywhere else where a tick might hide. Ticks need to be attached for 24–72 hours before they transmit most of the diseases that they carry, so you do have a window of opportunity for some preventative intervention.

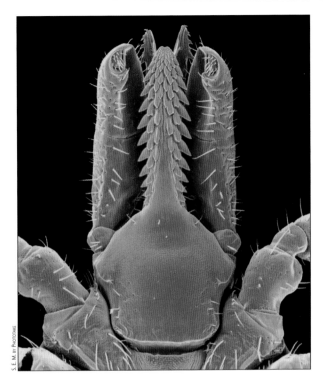

S. E. M. BY PHOTOTAKE

A scanning electron micrograph of the head of a female deer tick, *Ixodes dammini*, a parasitic tick that carries Lyme disease.

A TICKING BOMB

There is nothing good about a tick harpooning his nose into your dog's skin. Among the diseases caused by ticks are Rocky Mountain spotted fever, canine ehrlichiosis, canine babesiosis, canine hepatozoonosis and Lyme disease. If a dog is allergic to the saliva of a female wood tick, he can develop tick paralysis.

Female ticks live to eat and breed. They can lay between 4,000 and 5,000 eggs and they die soon after. Males, on the other hand, live only to mate with the females and continue the process as long as they are able. Most ticks live on multiple hosts before parasitizing dogs. The immature forms typically reside on grass and shrubs, waiting for suscep-tible animals to walk by. The larvae and nymph stages typically feed on wildlife.

If only a few ticks are present on a dog, they can be plucked out, but it is important to remove the entire head and mouthparts,

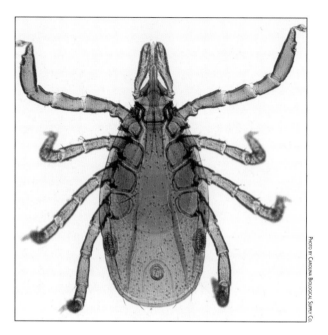

Deer tick,
Ixodes dammini.

disposed of in a container of alcohol or household bleach.

Some of the newer flea products, specifically those with fipronil, selamectin and permethrin, have effect against some, but not all, species of tick. Flea collars containing appropriate pesticides (e.g., propoxur, chlorfenvinphos) can aid in tick control. In most areas, such collars should be placed on animals in March, at the beginning of the tick season, and changed regularly. Leaving the collar on when the pesticide level is waning invites the development of resistance. Amitraz collars are also good for tick control, and the active ingredient does not interfere with other flea-control products. The ingredient helps prevent the attachment of ticks to the skin and will cause those ticks already on the skin to detach themselves.

which may be deeply embedded in the skin. This is best accomplished with forceps designed especially for this purpose; fingers can be used but should be protected with rubber gloves, plastic wrap or at least a paper towel. The tick should be grasped as closely as possible to the animal's skin and should be pulled upward with steady, even pressure. Do not squeeze, crush or puncture the body of the tick or you risk exposure to any disease carried by that tick. Once the ticks have been removed, the sites of attachment should be disinfected. Your hands should then be washed with soap and water to further minimize risk of contagion. The tick should be

TICK CONTROL
Removal of underbrush and leaf litter and the thinning of trees in areas where tick control is desired are recommended. These actions remove the cover and food sources for small animals that serve as hosts for ticks. With continued mowing of grasses in these areas, the probability of ticks' surviving is further reduced. A variety of insecticide ingredients (e.g., resmethrin, carbaryl, permethrin, chlorpyrifos, dioxathion and allethrin) are registered for tick control around the home.

MITES

Mites are tiny arachnid parasites that parasitize the skin of dogs. Skin diseases caused by mites are referred to as "mange," and there are many different forms seen in dogs. These forms are very different from one another, each one warranting an individual description.

Sarcoptic mange, or scabies, is one of the itchiest conditions that affects dogs. The microscopic *Sarcoptes* mites burrow into the superficial layers of the skin and can drive dogs crazy with itchiness. They are also communicable to people, although they can't complete their reproductive cycle on people. Not only are the mites tiny but also are often difficult to find when trying to make a diagnosis. Skin scrapings from multiple areas are examined microscopically but, even then, sometimes the mites cannot be found.

Fortunately, scabies is relatively easy to treat, and there are a variety of products that will successfully kill the mites. Since the mites can't live in the environment for very long without feeding, a complete cure is usually possible within four to eight weeks.

Cheyletiellosis is caused by a relatively large mite, which sometimes can be seen even without a microscope. Often referred to as "walking dandruff," this also causes itching, but not usually as profound as with scabies. While *Cheyletiella* mites can

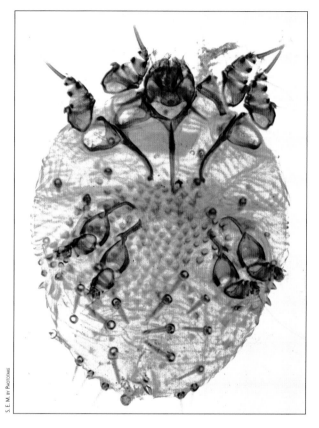

S. E. M. BY PHOTOTAKE

Sarcoptes scabiei, commonly known as the "itch mite."

survive somewhat longer in the environment than scabies mites, they too are relatively easy to treat, being responsive to not only the medications used to treat scabies but also often to flea-control products.

Otodectes cynotis, a mite that infests dogs' ears, is the cause of ear mites and is one of the more common causes of mange, especially in young dogs in shelters or pet stores. That's because the mites are typically present in large numbers and are quickly spread to

Micrograph of a dog louse, *Heterodoxus spiniger.* Female lice attach their eggs to the hairs of the dog. As the eggs hatch, the larval lice bite and feed on the blood. Lice can also feed on dead skin and hair, causing hair loss and skin problems for the dog.

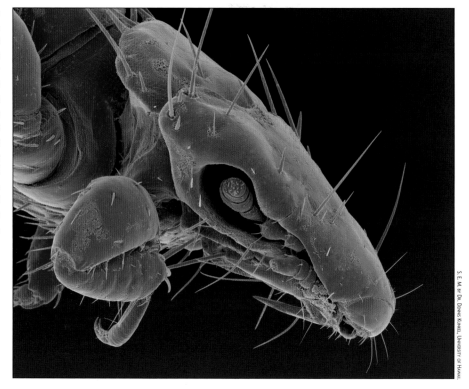

S. E. M. BY DR. DENNIS KUNKEL, UNIVERSITY OF HAWAII

nearby animals. The mites rarely do much harm but can be difficult to eradicate if the treatment regimen is not comprehensive. While many try to treat the condition with ear drops only, this is the most common cause of treatment failure. Ear drops cause the mites to simply move out of the ears and as far away as possible (usually to the base of the tail) until the insecticide levels in the ears drop to an acceptable level—then it's back to business as usual! The successful treatment of ear mites requires treating all animals in the household with a systemic insecticide, such as selamectin, or a combination of miticidal ear drops combined with whole-body flea-control preparations.

Demodicosis, sometimes referred to as red mange, can be one of the most difficult forms of mange to treat. Part of the problem has to do with the fact that the mites live in the hair follicles and they are relatively well shielded from topical and systemic products. The main issue, however, is that demodectic mange typically only results when there is some underlying process interfering with the dog's immune system.

Since *Demodex* mites are normal residents of the skin of mammals, including humans, there is usually a mite population explosion only when the immune system fails to keep the number of mites in check. In young animals, the immune deficit may be transient or may reflect an actual inherited immune problem. In older animals, demodicosis is usually seen only when there is another disease hampering the immune system, such as diabetes, cancer, thyroid problems or the use of immune-suppressing drugs. Accordingly, treatment involves not only trying to kill the mange mites but also discerning what is interfering with immune function and correcting it if possible.

Chiggers represent several different species of mite that don't parasitize dogs specifically, but do latch on to passersby and can cause irritation. The problem is most prevalent in wooded areas in the late summer and fall. Treatment is not difficult, as the mites do not complete their life cycle on dogs and are susceptible to a variety of miticidal products.

MOSQUITOES

Mosquitoes have long been known to transmit a variety of diseases to people, as well as just being biting pests during warm weather. They also pose a real risk to pets. Not only do they carry deadly heartworms but

ILLUSTRATION BY PHOTOTAKE

Illustration of *Demodex folliculoram.*

recently there also has been much concern over their involvement with West Nile virus. While we can avoid heartworm with the use of preventive medications, there are no such preventives for West Nile virus. The only method of prevention in endemic areas is active mosquito control. Fortunately, most dogs that have been exposed to the virus only developed flu-like symptoms and, to date, there have not been the large number of reported deaths in canines as seen in some other species.

MOSQUITO REPELLENT

Low concentrations of DEET (less than 10%), found in many human mosquito repellents, have been safely used in dogs but, in these concentrations, probably only give about two hours of protection. DEET may be safe in these small concentrations, but since it is not licensed for use on dogs, there is no research proving its safety for dogs. Products containing permethrin give the longest-lasting protection, perhaps two to four weeks. As DEET is not licensed for use on dogs, and both DEET and permethrin can be quite toxic to cats, appropriate care should be exercised. Other products, such as those containing oil of citronella, also have some mosquito-repellent activity, but typically have relatively short duration of action.

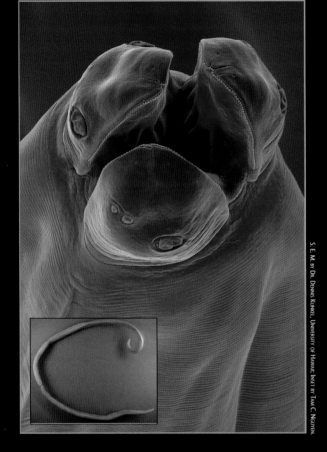

ASCARID DANGERS

The most commonly encountered worms in dogs are roundworms known as ascarids. *Toxascaris leonine* and *Toxocara canis* are the two species that infect dogs. Subsisting in the dog's stomach and intestines, adult roundworms can grow to 7 inches in length and adult females can lay in excess of 200,000 eggs in a single day.

In humans, visceral larval migrans affects people who have ingested eggs of *Toxocara canis*, which frequently contaminates children's sandboxes, beaches and park grounds. The roundworms reside in the human's stomach and intestines, as they would in a dog's, but do not mature. Instead, they find their way to the liver, lungs and skin, or even to the heart or kidneys in severe cases. Deworming puppies is critical in preventing the infection in humans, and young children should never handle nursing pups who have not been dewormed.

The ascarid roundworm *Toxocara canis,* showing the mouth with three lips. Inset: Photomicrograph of the roundworm *Ascaris lumbricoides.*

INTERNAL PARASITES: WORMS

ASCARIDS

Ascarids are intestinal roundworms that rarely cause severe disease in dogs. Nonetheless, they are of major public health significance because they can be transferred to people. Sadly, it is children who are most commonly affected by the parasite, probably from inadvertently ingesting ascarid-contaminated soil. In fact, many yards and children's sandboxes contain appreciable numbers of ascarid eggs. So, while ascarids don't bite dogs or latch onto their intestines to suck blood, they do cause some nasty medical conditions in children and are best eradicated from our furry friends. Because pups can start passing ascarid eggs by three weeks of age, most parasite-control programs begin at two weeks of age and are repeated every two weeks until pups are eight weeks old. It is important to

HOOKED ON ANCYLOSTOMA

Adult dogs can become infected by the bloodsucking nematodes we commonly call hookworms via ingesting larvae from the ground or via the larvae penetrating the dog's skin. It is not uncommon for infected dogs to show no symptoms of hookworm infestation. Sometimes symptoms occur within ten days of exposure. These symptoms can include bloody diarrhea, anemia, loss of weight and general weakness. Dogs pass the hookworm eggs in their stools, which serves as the vet's method of identifying the infestation. The hookworm larvae can encyst themselves in the dog's tissues and be released when the dog is experiencing stress.

Caused by an *Ancylostoma* species, whose common host is the dog, cutaneous larval migrans affects humans, causing itching and lumps and streaks beneath the surface of the skin.

S. E. M. BY DR. DENNIS KUNKEL, UNIVERSITY OF HAWAII.

realize that bitches can pass ascarids to their pups even if they test negative prior to whelping. Accordingly, bitches are best treated at the same time as the pups.

HOOKWORMS

Unlike ascarids, hookworms do latch onto a dog's intestinal tract and can cause significant loss of blood and protein. Similar to ascarids, hookworms can be transmitted to humans, where they cause a condition known as cutaneous larval migrans. Dogs can become infected either by consuming the infective larvae or by the larvae's penetrating the skin directly. People most often get infected when they are lying on the ground (such as on a beach) and the larvae penetrate the skin. Yes, the larvae can penetrate through a beach blanket. Hookworms are typically susceptible to the same medications used to treat ascarids.

The hookworm *Ancylostoma caninum* infects the colon of dogs. Inset: Note the row of hooks at the posterior end, used to anchor the worm to the intestinal wall.

WHIPWORMS

Whipworms latch onto the lower aspects of the dog's colon and can cause cramping and diarrhea. Eggs do not start to appear in the dog's feces until about three months after the dog was infected. This worm has a peculiar life cycle, which makes it more difficult to control than ascarids or hookworms. The good thing is that whipworms rarely are transferred to people.

Some of the medications used to treat ascarids and hookworms are also effective against whipworms, but, in general, a separate treatment protocol is needed. Since most of the medications are effective against the adults but not the eggs or larvae, treatment is typically repeated in three weeks, and then often in three

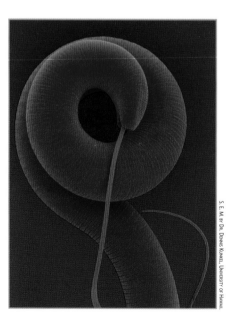

**Adult whipworm,
Trichuris sp.**

S. E. M. BY DR. DENNIS KUNKEL, UNIVERSITY OF HAWAII.

WORM-CONTROL GUIDELINES

• Practice sanitary habits with your dog and home.
• Clean up after your dog and don't let him sniff or eat other dogs' droppings.
• Control insects and fleas in the dog's environment. Fleas, lice, cockroaches, beetles, mice and rats can act as hosts for various worms.
• Prevent dogs from eating uncooked meat, raw poultry and dead animals.
• Keep dogs and children from playing in sand and soil.
• Kennel dogs on cement or gravel; avoid dirt runs.
• Administer heartworm preventatives regularly.
• Have your vet examine your dog's stools at your annual visits.
• Select a boarding kennel carefully, so as to avoid contamination from other dogs or an unsanitary environment.
• Prevent dogs from roaming. Obey local leash laws.

---

months as well. Unfortunately, since dogs don't develop resistance to whipworms, it is difficult to prevent them from getting reinfected if they visit soil contaminated with whipworm eggs.

TAPEWORMS

There are many different species of tapeworm that affect dogs, but *Dipylidium caninum* is probably the most common and is spread by

---

fleas. Flea larvae feed on organic debris and tapeworm eggs in the environment and, when a dog chews at himself and manages to ingest fleas, he might get a dose of tapeworm at the same time. The tapeworm then develops further in the intestine of the dog.

The tapeworm itself, which latches onto the intestinal wall, is composed of numerous segments. When the segments break off into the intestine (as proglottids), they may accumulate around the rectum, like grains of rice. While this tapeworm is disgusting in its behavior, it is not directly communicable to humans (although humans can also get infected by swallowing fleas).

A much more dangerous flatworm is *Echinococcus multilocularis*, which is typically found in foxes, coyotes and wolves. The eggs are passed in the feces and infect rodents, and, when dogs eat the rodents, the dogs can be infected by thousands of adult tapeworms. While the parasites don't cause many problems in dogs, this is considered the most lethal worm infection that people can get. Take appropriate precautions if you live in an area in which these tapeworms are found. Do not use mulch that may contain feces of dogs, cats or wildlife, and discourage your pets from hunting wildlife. Treat these tapeworm infections aggressively in pets, because if humans get infected, approximately half die.

HEARTWORMS

Heartworm disease is caused by the parasite *Dirofilaria immitis* and is seen in dogs around the world. The parasite itself, another nematode, is spread between dogs by the bite of an infected mosquito. The mosquito injects infective larvae into the dog's skin with its bite, and these larvae develop under the skin for a period of time before making their way to the heart. There they develop into adults, which grow and create blockages of the heart, lungs and major blood vessels there. They also start producing offspring (microfilariae)

Dog tapeworm proglottid.

Dog tapeworm, *Taenia pisiformis*.

A Look at Internal Parasites

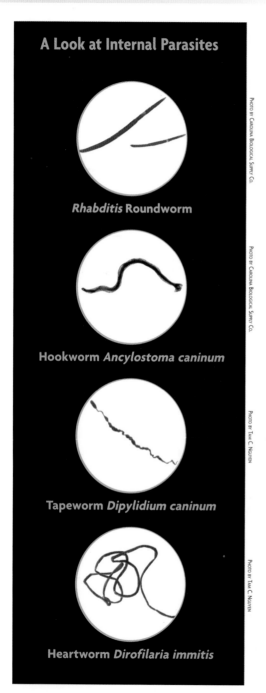

Rhabditis Roundworm

Hookworm *Ancylostoma caninum*

Tapeworm *Dipylidium caninum*

Heartworm *Dirofilaria immitis*

PHOTO BY CAROLINA BIOLOGICAL SUPPLY CO.

PHOTO BY CAROLINA BIOLOGICAL SUPPLY CO.

PHOTO BY TAM C. NGUYEN

PHOTO BY TAM C. NGUYEN

and these microfilariae circulate in the bloodstream, waiting to hitch a ride when the next mosquito bites. Once in the mosquito, the microfilariae develop into infective larvae and the entire process is repeated.

When dogs get infected with heartworm, over time they tend to develop symptoms associated with heart disease, such as coughing, exercise intolerance and potentially many other manifestations. Diagnosis is confirmed by either seeing the microfilariae themselves in blood samples or using immunologic tests (antigen testing) to identify the presence of adult heartworms. Since antigen tests measure the presence of adult heartworms and microfilarial tests measure offspring produced by adults, neither are positive until six to seven months after the initial infection. However, the beginning of damage can occur by fifth-stage larvae as early as three months after infection. Thus it is possible for dogs to be harboring problem-causing larvae for up to three months before either type of test would identify an infection.

The good news is that there are great protocols available for preventing heartworm in dogs. Testing is critical in the process, and it is important to understand the benefits as well as the limitations of such testing. All dogs six months of age or older that have not been on continuous heartworm-preventive medication should be

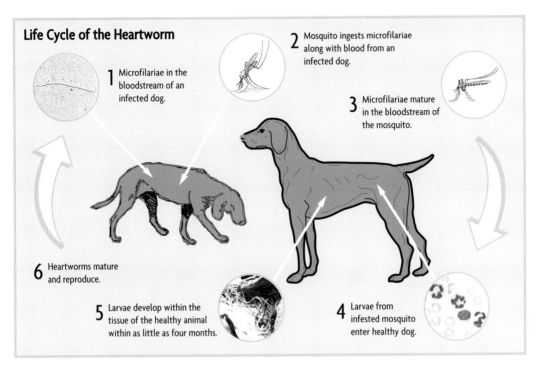

Life Cycle of the Heartworm

1 Microfilariae in the bloodstream of an infected dog.

2 Mosquito ingests microfilariae along with blood from an infected dog.

3 Microfilariae mature in the bloodstream of the mosquito.

4 Larvae from infested mosquito enter healthy dog.

5 Larvae develop within the tissue of the healthy animal within as little as four months.

6 Heartworms mature and reproduce.

screened with microfilarial or antigen tests. For dogs receiving preventive medication, periodic antigen testing helps assess the effectiveness of the preventives. The American Heartworm Society guidelines suggest that annual retesting may not be necessary when owners have absolutely provided continuous heartworm prevention. Retesting on a two- to three-year interval may be sufficient in these cases. However, your veterinarian will likely have specific guidelines under which heartworm preventives will be prescribed, and many prefer to err on the side of safety and retest annually.

It is indeed fortunate that heartworm is relatively easy to prevent, because treatments can be as life-threatening as the disease itself. Treatment requires a two-step process that kills the adult heartworms first and then the microfilariae. Prevention is obviously preferable; this involves a once-monthly oral or topical treatment. The most common oral preventives include ivermectin (not suitable for some breeds), moxidectin and milbemycin oxime; the once-a-month topical drug selamectin provides heartworm protection in addition to flea, tick and other parasite controls.

BASSET FAUVE DE BRETAGNE

When we bring home a puppy, full of the energy and exuberance that accompanies youth, we hope for a long, happy and fulfilling relationship with the new family member. Even when we adopt an older dog, we look forward to the years of companionship ahead with a new canine friend. However, aging is inevitable for all creatures, and there will come a time when our dog reaches his senior years and will need special consideration and attention to his care.

WHEN IS MY DOG A "SENIOR"?

Dogs generally are considered "seniors" at seven years of age, but that is not always accurate. A dog's senior status is better determined based on the average life expectancy for his breed, which is based on the size of the breed. Average life expectancies are considered as follows: Small breeds, 12 years or more; medium breeds, 10 years or more; large breeds, 9 years or more and giant breeds, 7 years or more. A dog is considered a senior when he has reached 75% of the average

lifespan for his breed. Your Basset Fauve has an average lifespan of 12-14 years and thus is a senior citizen at around 9 or 10.

The old "seven dog years to one human year" theory is not exact. In puppyhood, a dog's year is actually comparable to more than seven human years, considering the puppy's rapid growth during his first year. Then, in adulthood, the ratio decreases. Regardless, a more viable rule of thumb is that the larger the dog, the shorter his expected lifespan. Of course, this can vary among individual dogs, with many living longer than expected, which we hope is the case!

WHAT ARE THE SIGNS OF AGING?

By the time your dog has reached his senior years, you will know him very well and, thus, the physical and behavioral changes that accompany aging should be noticeable to you. Humans and dogs share the most obvious physical sign of aging: gray hair! Graying often occurs first on the muzzle and face, around the eyes. Other telltale signs are the dog's overall decrease in activity. Your older dog might be more content to nap and rest, and he may not show the same old enthusiasm when it's time to play in the yard or go for a walk. Other physical signs include significant weight loss or gain; more labored movement; skin and coat problems, possibly hair loss; sight and/or hearing problems; changes in toileting habits, perhaps seeming "unhousebroken" at times; tooth decay, bad breath or other mouth problems.

There are behavioral changes that go along with aging, too. There are numerous causes for behavioral changes. Sometimes a dog's apparent confusion results from a physical change like diminished sight or hearing. If his confusion causes him to be afraid, he may act aggressively or defensively. He may sleep more frequently because his daily walks, though shorter now, tire him out. He may begin to experience separation anxiety or, conversely, become less interested in petting and attention.

There also are clinical conditions that cause behavioral changes in older dogs. One such condition is known as canine cognitive dysfunction (familiarly known as "old-dog" syndrome). It can be frustrating for an owner whose dog is affected with cognitive dysfunction, as it can result in behavioral changes of all types, most seemingly unexplainable. Common changes include the dog's forgetting aspects of the daily routine, such as times to eat,

AH, MY ACHING BONES!

As your pet ages and things that once were routine become difficult for him to handle, you may need to make some adjustments around the home to make things easier for your dog. Senior dogs affected by arthritis may have trouble moving about. If you notice this in your dog, you may have to limit him to one floor of the house so that he does not have to deal with stairs. If there are a few steps leading out into the yard, a ramp may help the dog. Likewise, he may need a ramp or a boost to get in and out of the car. Ensure that he has plenty of soft bedding on which to sleep and rest, as this will be comfortable for his aching joints. Also ensure that surfaces on which the dog walks are not slippery.

Investigate new dietary supplements made for arthritic dogs. Studies have found that products containing glucosamine added once or twice daily to the senior dog's food can have beneficial effects on the dog's joints. Many of these products also contain natural anti-inflammatories such as chondroitin, MSM and cetyl myristoleate, as well as natural herbal remedies and nutmeg. Talk to your vet about these supplements.

go out for walks, relieve himself and the like. Along the same lines, you may take your dog out at the regular time for a potty trip and he may have no idea why he is there. Sometimes a placid dog will begin to show aggressive or possessive tendencies or, conversely, a hyperactive dog will start to "mellow out."

Disease also can be the cause of behavioral changes in senior dogs. Hormonal problems (Cushing's disease is common in older dogs), diabetes and thyroid disease can cause increased appetite, which can lead to aggression related to food guarding. It's better to be proactive with your senior dog, making more frequent trips to the vet if necessary and having bloodwork done to test for the diseases that can commonly befall the older Basset Fauve.

This is not to say that, as dogs age, they all fall apart physically and become nasty in personality. The aforementioned changes are discussed to alert owners to the things that may happen as their dogs get older. Many hardy dogs remain active and alert well into old age. However, it can be frustrating and heartbreaking for owners to see their beloved dogs change physically and tempera-mentally. Just know that it's the same dog under there and that he still loves you and appreciates your care, which he needs now more than ever.

HOW DO I CARE FOR MY AGING DOG?

Again, every dog is an individual in terms of aging. Your dog might reach the estimated "senior" age for his breed and show no signs of slowing down. However, even if he shows no outward signs of aging, he should begin a senior-care program once he reaches the determined age. He may not show it, but he's not a pup anymore! By providing him with extra attention to his veterinary care at this age, you will be practicing good preventive medicine, ensuring that the rest of your dog's life will be as long, active, happy and healthy as possible. If you do notice indications of aging, such as graying and/or changes in sleeping, eating or toileting habits, this is a sign to set up a senior-care visit with your vet right away to make sure that these changes are not related to any health problems.

To start, senior dogs should visit the vet twice yearly for exams, routine tests and overall evaluations. Many veterinarians have special screening programs especially for senior dogs that can include a thorough physical exam; blood test to determine complete blood count; serum biochemistry test, which screens for liver, kidney and blood problems as well as cancer; urinalysis; and dental exams. With these tests, it can be determined if your dog has

As dogs get older, they have less desire to run and play and are more content to find a comfy spot to rest.

any health problems; the results also establish a baseline for your pet against which future test results can be compared.

In addition to these tests, your vet may suggest additional testing, including an EKG, tests for glaucoma and other problems of the eye, chest X-rays, screening for tumors, blood pressure test, test for thyroid function and screening for parasites and reassessment of his preventive program. Your vet also will ask you questions about your dog's diet and activity level, what you feed and the amounts that you feed. This information, along with his evaluation of the dog's overall condition, will enable him to suggest proper dietary changes, if needed.

This may seem like quite a work-up for your pet, but veterinarians advise that older dogs need more frequent attention so

that any health problems can be detected as early as possible. Serious conditions like kidney disease, heart disease and cancer may not present outward symptoms, or the problem may go undetected if the symptoms are mistaken by owners as just part of the aging process.

There are some conditions more common in the elderly dogs that are difficult to ignore. Cognitive dysfunction shares much in common with senility and Alzheimer's disease, and dogs are not immune. Dogs can become confused and/or disoriented, lose their house-training, have abnormal sleep-wake cycles and interact differently with their owners. Be heartened by the fact that, in some ways, there are more treatment options for dogs with cognitive dysfunction than for people with similar conditions. There is good evidence that continued stimula-

ADAPTING TO AGE

As dogs age and their once-keen senses begin to deteriorate, they can experience stress and confusion. However, dogs are very adaptable, and most can adjust to deficiencies in their sight and hearing. As these processes often deteriorate gradually, the dog makes adjustments gradually, too. Because dogs become so familiar with the layout of their homes and yards, and with their daily routines, they are able to get around even if they cannot see or hear as well. Help your senior dog by keeping things consistent around the house. Keep up with your regular times for walking and potty trips, and do not relocate his crate or rearrange the furniture. Your dog is a very adaptable creature and can make compensation for his diminished ability, but you want to help him along the way and not make changes that will cause him confusion.

tion in the form of games, play, training and exercise can help to maintain cognitive function. There are also medications (such as seligi-line) and antioxidant-fortified senior diets that have been shown to be beneficial.

Cancer is also a condition more common in the elderly. Almost all of the cancers seen in people are also seen in pets. While we can't control the effects of second-hand smoke, lung cancer, which is a major killer in humans, is relatively rare in dogs. If pets are getting regular physical examinations, cancers are often detected early. There are a variety of cancer therapies available today and many pets continue to live happy lives with appropriate treatment.

Degenerative joint disease, often referred to as arthritis, is another common malady shared between elderly dogs and humans. A lifetime of wear and tear on joints, and running around at play, eventually takes its toll and results in stiffness and difficulty getting around. As dogs live longer and healthier lives, it is natural that they should eventually feel some of the effects of aging. Once again, if regular veterinary care has been available, your pet was not carrying extra pounds all those years and wearing those joints out before their time. If your pet was unfortunate enough to inherit hip dysplasia, osteochondrosis dissecans, or any of the other developmental orthopedic diseases, battling the onset of degenerative joint disease was probably a longstanding goal. In any case, there are now many effective remedies for managing degenerative joint disease and a number of remarkable surgeries as well.

Aside from the extra veterinary care, there is much you can do at home to keep your older dog in good condition. The dog's diet is an important factor. If your dog's appetite decreases, he will not be getting the nutrients he needs. He also will lose weight, which is unhealthy for a dog at a proper weight. Conversely, an older dog's metabolism is slower and he usually exercises less, but he should not be allowed to become obese. Obesity in an older dog is especially risky, because extra pounds mean extra stress on the body, increasing his vulnerability to heart disease. Plus, the additional pounds make it harder for the dog to move about.

You should discuss age-related feeding changes with your vet. For a dog who has lost interest in food, it may be suggested to try some different types of food until you find something new that the dog likes. For an obese dog, a "light" formula dog food or reducing food portions may be advised, along with exercise appropriate to his physical condition and energy level.

As for exercise, despite his old age, the senior dog should not be allowed to become a "couch potato." He may not be able to handle the morning run, long walks and vigorous games of fetch, but he still needs to get up and get moving. Keep up with your daily walks, but keep the distances shorter, and let your dog set the pace. If he gets to the point where he's not up for walks, let him stroll around the yard. On the other hand, many dogs remain very active in their senior years, so base changes to the exercise program on your own individual dog and what he's capable of. Don't worry, your dog will let you know when it's time to rest.

Keep up with your grooming routine as you always have. Be extra diligent about checking the skin and coat for problems. Older dogs can experience thinning coats as a normal aging process, but they can also lose hair as a result of medical problems. Some thinning is normal, but patches of baldness or the loss of significant amounts of hair is not.

Hopefully, you've been regular with brushing your dog's teeth throughout his life. Healthy teeth directly affect overall good health. We already know that bacteria from gum infections can enter the dog's body through the damaged gums and travel to the organs. At a stage in life when his organs don't function as well as they used to, you don't want anything to put additional strain on them. Clean teeth also contribute to a healthy immune system. Offering the dental-type chews in addition to toothbrushing can help, as they remove plaque and tartar as the dog chews.

Along with the same good care you've given him all of his life, pay a little extra attention to your dog in his senior years and keep up with twice-yearly trips to the vet. The sooner a problem is uncovered, the greater the chances of a full recovery.

BEHAVIOR OF YOUR

BASSET FAUVE DE BRETAGNE

Bassets Fauves are known for being friendly dogs, brimming with personality, as aptly demonstrated by this smiling pair and friends.

You chose your dog because something clicked the minute you set eyes on him. Or perhaps it seemed that the dog selected you! Either way, you are now investing time and money in this dog, a true pal and an outstanding member of the family. Everything about him is perfect…well, *almost*. Remember, he is a dog! For that matter, how does he think you're doing?

UNDERSTANDING THE CANINE MINDSET

For starters, you and your dog are on different wavelengths. Your dog is similar to a toddler in that both live in the present tense only. A dog's view of life is based primarily on cause and effect, which is similar to the old saying, "Nothing teaches a youngster to hang on like falling off the swing." If your dog stumbles down a flight of three steps, the next time he will try the Superman approach and fling himself off the top one!

Your dog makes connections based on the fact that he lives in the present, so when he is doing something and you interrupt to dispense praise or a correction, a connection, positive or negative, is made. To the dog, that's like one plus one equals two! In the same sense, it's also easy to see that when your timing is off, you will cause an incorrect connection. The one-plus-one way of thinking is why you must never scold a dog for behavior that took place an hour, 15 minutes or even

15 seconds ago. But it is also why, when your timing is perfect, you can teach him to do all kinds of wonderful things—as soon as he has made that essential connection. What helps the process is his desire to please you and to have your approval.

There are behaviors we admire in dogs, such as friendliness and obedience, as well as those behaviors that cause problems to a varying degree. The dog owner who encounters minor behavior problems is wise to solve them promptly or get professional help. Bad behaviors are not corrected by repeatedly shouting "No" or getting angry with the dog. Only praise and approval for good behavior lets your dog understand right from wrong. The longer a bad behavior is allowed to continue, the harder it is to overcome. A responsible breeder is often able to help. Each dog is unique, even within a specific breed, so try not to compare your dog's behavior with your neighbor's dog or the one you had as a child.

Have your veterinarian check the dog to see if a behavior problem could have a physical cause. An earache or toothache, for example, could be the reason for a dog to snap at you if you were to touch his head when putting on his leash. A sharp correction from you would only increase the behavior. When a physical basis is eliminated, and if the problem is not something you

> **GET A WHIFF OF HIM!**
> Dogs sniff each others' rears as their way of saying "hi" as well as to find out who the other dog is and how he's doing. That's normal behavior between canines, but it can, annoyingly, extend to people. The command for all unwanted sniffing is "Leave it!" Give the command in a no-nonsense voice and move on.

understand or can cope with, ask for the name of a behavioral specialist, preferably one who is familiar with the Basset Fauve. Be sure to keep the breeder informed of your progress.

Many things, such as environment and inherited traits, form the basic behavior of a dog, just as in humans. You also must factor into his temperament the purpose for which your dog was originally bred. The major obstacle lies in the dog's inability to explain his behavior to us in a way that we understand. The one thing you should not do is to give up and abandon your dog. Somewhere a misunderstanding has occurred but, with help and patient understanding on your part, you should be able to work out the majority of bothersome behaviors.

AGGRESSION

This is a problem that concerns all responsible dog owners, even owners of breeds like the Basset Fauve, which are not known for

THE TOP-DOG TUG

When puppies play tug-o-war, the dominant pup wins. Children also play this kind of game but, for their own safety, must be prevented from ever engaging in this type of play with their dogs. Playing tug-o-war games can result in a dog's developing aggressive behavior. Don't be the cause of such behavior.

being aggressive toward people or other dogs. Nonetheless, aggression can be a problem in dogs of any breed, and, when not controlled, always becomes dangerous. An aggressive dog may lunge at, bite or even attack a person or another dog. Aggressive behavior is not to be tolerated. It is more than just inappropriate behavior; it is painful for a family to watch their dog become unpredictable in his behavior to the point where they are afraid of him. While not all aggressive behaviors are dangerous, things like growling, baring teeth, etc., can be frightening. It is important to ascertain why the dog is acting in this

manner. Aggression is a display of dominance, and the dog should not have the dominant role in its pack, which is, in this case, your family.

It is important not to challenge an aggressive dog, as this could provoke an attack. Observe your Basset Fauve's body language. Does he make direct eye contact and stare? Does he try to make himself as large as possible: ears pricked, chest out, tail erect? Height and size signify authority in a dog pack—being taller or "above" another dog literally means that he is "above" in social status. These body signals tell you that your Basset Fauve thinks he is in charge, a problem that needs to be addressed. An aggressive dog is unpredictable; you never know when he is going to strike and what he is going to do. You cannot understand why a dog that is playful one minute is growling the next.

Fear is a common cause of aggression in dogs. Perhaps your Basset Fauve had a negative experience as a puppy, which causes him to be fearful when a similar situation presents itself later in life. The dog may act aggressively in order to protect himself from whatever is making him afraid. It is not always easy to determine what is making your dog fearful, but if you can isolate what brings out the fear reaction, you can help the dog get over it. Supervise your Basset Fauve's interactions with people and other dogs, and praise the dog when it goes well. If he starts to act aggressively in a situation, correct him and remove him from the situation. Do not let people approach the dog and start petting him without your express permission. That way you can have the dog sit to accept petting, and praise him when he behaves properly. You are focusing on praise and on modifying his behavior by rewarding him when he acts appropriately. By being gentle and by supervising his interactions, you are showing him that there is no need to be afraid or defensive.

The best solution is to consult a behavioral specialist, one who is familiar with the breed or similar breeds. Together, perhaps you can pinpoint the cause of your dog's aggression and do something about it. An aggressive dog cannot be trusted, and a dog that cannot be trusted is not safe to have as a family pet. If, very unusually, you find that your pet has become untrustworthy and you feel it necessary to seek a new home with a more suitable family and environment, explain fully to the new owners all your reasons for rehoming the dog to be fair to all concerned.

SEPARATION ANXIETY

Any behaviorist will tell you that separation anxiety is the most common problem about which pet owners complain. It is also one of the easiest to prevent, or even to correct. Unfortunately, a behaviorist usually is not consulted until the dog is a stressed-out, neurotic mess. At that stage, it is indeed a problem that requires the help of a professional.

Training the puppy to the fact that people in the house come and go is essential in order to avoid this anxiety. Leaving the puppy in his crate or a confined area while family members go in and out, and stay out for longer and longer periods of time, is the basic way to desensitize the pup to the family's frequent departures. If you are at home most of every day, make it a point to go out for at least an hour or two whenever possible.

How you leave is vital to the dog's reaction. Your dog is no fool. He knows the difference between sweats and business suits, jeans and dresses. He sees you pat your pocket to check for your wallet, open your briefcase, check that you have your cell phone or pick up

HAND-SHY
A puppy will shy away when a hand comes down onto his head. To the pup, this is a threatening gesture, not a welcome pat. Older dogs shy from the same hand gesture because it's a dominant move on the part of the human. The best way to approach a dog is by crouching down and holding out your hand, palm up, for him to sniff.

While your Basset Fauve will thoroughly enjoy time spent outdoors, don't forget that he needs to spend time in the home, doing things with the family and being part of family activities.

can watch you leave the house. If you're leaving for an hour or two, just put him in his crate with a safe toy.

Now comes the test! You are ready to walk out the door. Do not give your dog a big hug and a fond farewell. Do not drag out a long goodbye. Those are the very things that jump-start separation anxiety. Toss a biscuit into the dog's area, call out "So long, pooch" and close the door. You're gone. The chances are that the dog may bark a couple of times, or maybe whine once or twice, and then settle down to enjoy his biscuit and take a lovely nap, especially if you took him for a nice long walk after breakfast. As he grows up, the barks and whines

the car keys. He knows from the hurry of the kids in the morning that they're off to school until afternoon. Lipstick? Aftershave lotion? Lunch boxes? Every move you make registers in his sensory perception and memory. Your puppy knows more about your departure than the FBI. You can't get away with a thing!

Before you got dressed, you checked the dog's water bowl and his supply of toys (including a long-lasting chew toy), and turned the radio on low. You will leave him in what he considers his "safe" area, not with total freedom of the house. If you've invested in child safety gates, you can be reasonably sure that he'll remain in the designated area. Don't give him access to a window where he

EXIT STAGE LEFT

Your dog studies your every move. He knows that before you leave the house, you gather a bunch of stuff, put on your coat and shake your keys. His anxiety emerges at the first sight of seeing you begin your "exit routine." If your dog suffers from separation anxiety, you should rethink your exit. Mix up your routine and include your dog in some of the tasks. Play a short game of fetch, reward the dog for a couple of commands, present him with a fun, safe toy and give him a treat before you leave the house. If the dog is exercised, content and focused on something other than your exit, he may learn to adapt better to your absence.

will stop because it's an old routine, so why should he make the effort?

When you first brought home the puppy, the come-and-go routine was intermittent and constant. He was put in his crate with a tiny treat. You left (silently) and returned in 3 minutes, then 5, then 10, then 15, then half an hour, until finally you could leave without a problem and be gone for two or three hours. If, at any time in the future, there's a "separation" problem, refresh his memory by going back to that basic training.

Now comes the next most important part—your return. Do not make a big production of coming home. "Hi, poochie" is as grand a greeting as he needs. When you've taken off your hat and coat, tossed your briefcase on the hall table and glanced at the mail, and the dog has settled down from the excitement of seeing you "in person" from his confined area, then go and give him a warm, friendly greeting. A potty trip is needed and a walk would be appreciated, since he's been such a good dog.

DIGGING

Digging, which is seen as a destructive behavior to humans, is actually quite a natural behavior in dogs. Although terriers (the "earth dogs") are most associated with digging, any dog's desire to

dig can be irrepressible and most frustrating to his owners. Bassets Fauves can develop a destructive digging habit if left for hours on end without a job to do. Boredom is usually to blame, as opposed to the need to escape or the pursuit of vermin. The dog feels useful when he digs. Thus, when digging occurs in your lawn, it is actually a normal behavior redirected into something the dog can do in his everyday life. In the wild, a dog would be actively seeking food, making his own shelter, etc. He would be using his paws in a purposeful manner for his survival. Since you provide him with food and shelter, he has no need to use his paws for these purposes, so the energy that he would be using may manifest itself in the form of little holes all over your yard and flower beds.

To eliminate boredom digging, provide the dog with adequate play and exercise so that his mind and paws are occupied, and so

Digging is more fun with a friend, and these two are investigating a possible excavation site.

that he feels as if he is doing something useful. Digging is easiest to control if it is stopped as soon as possible, but it is often hard to catch a dog in the act. If your dog is a compulsive digger and is not easily distracted by other activities, you can designate an area on your property where he is allowed to dig. If you catch him digging in an off-limits area of the yard, immediately bring him to the approved area and praise him for digging there. Keep a close eye on him so that you can catch him in the act—-that is the only way to make him understand what is permitted and what is not. If you take him to a hole he dug an hour ago and tell him "No," he will understand that you are not fond of holes, dirt or flowers. If you catch him while he is stifle-deep in your tulips, that is when he will get your message.

QUIET DOWN!

If your dog barks excessively, don't bark back. Yelling at him only encourages him to keep it up. Barking at the garbage truck makes perfect sense to the dog—that man is stealing your garbage! When the garbage truck leaves, that spells success to the dog: he has scared away the garbage man with his bark! Pick a command word, something like "Quiet" or "No Bark," to stop his barking. The second he stops, tell him "Good dog" and toss him a toy.

BARKING

The Basset Fauve does not have the musical voice of his cousin, the Basset Hound. Like most other dogs, Bassets Fauves will bark from time to time, but not excessively so. They usually will use their bark to alert their owners about visitors to the home. Barking is your dog's means of letting you know that there is an intrusion, whether friend or foe, on your property. This type of barking is instinctive and should not be discouraged.

Excessive habitual barking, however, is a problem that should be corrected early on. As your Basset Fauve grows up, you will be able to tell when his barking is purposeful and when it is for no reason. You will become able to distinguish your dog's different barks and their meanings. For example, the bark when someone comes to the door will be different from the bark when he is excited to see you. It is similar to a person's tone of voice, except that the dog has to rely totally on tone of voice because he does not have the benefit of using words. An incessant barker will be evident at an early age.

There are some things that encourage a dog to bark. For example, if your dog barks non-stop for a few minutes and you give him a treat to quiet him, he believes that you are rewarding him for barking. He will associate barking with getting a treat and will keep doing it until he is rewarded. On the other hand, if you give him a command such as "Quiet" and praise him after he has stopped barking for a few seconds, he will get the idea that being "quiet" is what you want him to do.

MATTERS OF SEX

For whatever reasons, real or imagined, most people tend to have a preference in choosing between a male or female puppy. Some, but not all, of the undesirable traits attributed to the sex of the dog can be suppressed by early spaying or neutering. The major advantage, of course, is that a neutered male or a spayed female will not be adding to the overpopulation of dogs.

An unaltered male will mark territory by lifting his leg everywhere, leaving a few drops of urine indoors on your furniture and appliances, and outside on everything he passes. It is difficult to catch him in the act, because he only leaves a few drops each time, but it is very hard to eliminate the odor. Thus the cycle begins, because the odor will entice him to mark that spot again.

If you have bought a bitch with the intention of breeding her, be sure you know what you are getting into. She will go through one or two periods of estrus each year, each cycle lasting about

THE MACHO DOG

The Venus/Mars differences are found in dogs, too. Males have distinct behaviors that, while seemingly sex-related, are more closely connected to the role of the male as leader. Marking territory by urinating on it is one means that male dogs use to establish their presence. Doing so merely says, "I've been here." Small dogs often attempt to lift their legs higher on the tree than the previous male. While this is natural behavior outdoors on items like telephone poles, fence posts, fire hydrants and most other upright objects, marking indoors is totally unacceptable. Treat it as you would a house-training accident and clean thoroughly to eradicate the scent. Another behavior often seen in the macho male, mounting is a dominance display. Neutering the dog before six months of age helps to deter this behavior. You can discourage him from mounting by catching the dog as he's about to mount you, stepping quickly aside and saying "Off!"

At 12 weeks old, this pup is looking for anything he can sink his teeth into! Supervision and directing his chewing onto proper objects are essential during the teething stage.

it to each other and adults do it regardless of sex, because it is not so much a sexual act as it is one of dominance. It becomes very annoying when the dog mounts your legs, the kids or the couch cushions; in these and any other instances of mounting, he should be corrected. Touching sometimes stimulates the dog, so pulling the dog off by his collar or leash, together with a consistent and stern "Off!" command, usually eliminates the behavior.

CHEWING

All puppies chew. All dogs chew. This is a fact of life for canines, and sometimes you may think it's what your dog does best. A pup starts chewing when his first set of teeth erupts and continues throughout the teething period. Chewing gives the pup relief from itchy gums and incoming teeth and, from that time on, he gets great satisfaction out of this normal, somewhat idle, canine activity. Providing safe chew toys is the best way to direct this behavior in an appropriate manner. Chew toys are available in all sizes, textures and flavors, but you must monitor the wear-and-tear inflicted on your pup's toys to be sure that the ones you've chosen are safe and remain in good condition.

three weeks. During these times, she will have to be kept confined to protect your furniture and to protect her from being bred by a male other than the one you have selected. Breeding should never be undertaken to "show the kids the miracle of birth." Bitches can die giving birth, and the puppies may also die. The dam often exhibits what is called "maternal aggression" after the pups are born. Her intention is to protect her pups, but in fact she can be extremely vicious. Breeding should be left to the experienced breeders, who do so for the betterment of the breed and with much research and planning behind each mating.

Mounting is not unusual in dogs, male or female. Puppies do

Puppies cannot distinguish between a rawhide toy and a nice

leather shoe or wallet. It's up to you to keep your possessions away from the dog and to keep your eye on the dog. There's a form of destruction caused by chewing that is not the dog's fault. Let's say you allow him on the sofa. One day he takes a rawhide bone up on the sofa and, in the course of chewing on the bone, takes up a bit of fabric. He continues to chew. Disaster! Now you've learned the lesson: dogs with chew toys have either to be kept off furniture and carpets, carefully supervised or put in their confined areas for chew time.

The wooden legs of furniture are favorite objects for chewing. The first time, tell the dog "Leave it!" (or "No!") and offer him a chew toy as a substitute. But your clever dog may be hiding under the chair and doing some silent destruction, which you may not notice until it's too late. In this case, it's time to try one of the foul-tasting products, made specifically to prevent destructive chewing, that are sprayed on the objects of your dog's chewing attention. These products also work to keep the dog away from plants, trash, etc. It's even a good way to stop the dog from "mouthing" or chewing on your hands or the leg of your pants. (Be sure to wash your hands after the mouthing lesson!) A little spray goes a long way.

No one can deny that a dog's jumping up to say hi is adorable, so that may be why some owners are reluctant to correct the behavior.

JUMPING UP

Jumping up is a device of enthusiastic, attention-seeking puppies, but adult dogs often like to jump up as well, usually as a form of canine greeting. This is a controversial issue. Some owners wouldn't have it any other way! They encourage their dogs, and the owners and dogs alike enjoy the friendly physical contact. Certain breeds are even renowned for this behavior. In some breeds, it's cute when it comes from a puppy, but not from an adult that weighs over 100 pounds!

Conversely, there are those who consider jumping up to be one of the worst kinds of bad manners to be found in a dog. Among this group inevitably are bound to be some of your best friends. There are two situations in which your dog should be restrained from any and all jumping up. One is around children, especially young children and those who are not at ease with dogs. The other is when you are entertaining guests. No one who comes dressed up for a party wants to be groped by your dog, no matter how friendly his intentions or how clean his paws.

The answer to this one is relatively simple. If the dog has already started to jump up, the first command is "Off," followed immediately by "Sit." The dog must sit every time you are about to meet a friend on the street or when someone enters your home, be it child or adult. You may have to ask people to ignore the dog for a few minutes in order to let his urge for an enthusiastic greeting subside. If your dog is too exuberant and won't sit still, you'll have to work harder by first telling him "Off" and then issuing the down-stay command. This requires more work on your part, because the down is a submissive position and your dog is only trying to be super-friendly. A small treat is expected when training for this particular down.

If you have a real pet peeve about dogs' jumping up, then do not allow it from the day your puppy comes home. Jumping up is a subliminally taught human-to-dog greeting. Dogs don't greet each other in this way. It begins because your puppy is close to the ground and he's easier to pet and cuddle if he reaches up and you bend over to meet him halfway. If you won't like it later, don't start it when he is young, but do give lots of praise and affection for a good sit.

FOOD-RELATED PROBLEMS

We're not talking about eating, diets or nutrition here, we're talking about bad habits. Face it. All dogs are beggars. Food is the motivation for everything we want our dogs to do and, when you combine that with their innate ability to "con" us in order to get their way, it's a wonder there aren't far more obese dogs in the world.

Who can resist the bleeding-heart look that says "I'm starving," or the paw that gently pats your knee and gives you a knowing look, or the whining "please" or even the total body language of a perfect sit beneath the cookie jar. No one who professes to love his dog can turn down the pleas of his clever canine's performances every time. One thing is for sure, though: definitely do not allow begging at the table. Family meals do not include your dog.

Control your dog's begging habit by making your dog work for his rewards. Ignore his begging when you can. Utilize the obedience commands you've taught your dog. Use "Off" for the pawing. A sit or even a long down will interrupt the whining. His reward in these situations is definitely not a treat! Casual verbal praise is enough. Be sure all members of the family follow the same rules. There is a different type of begging that does demand your immediate response and that is the appeal to be let (or taken) outside! Usually that is a quick paw or small whine to get your attention, followed by a race to the door. This type of begging needs your quick attention and approval. Of course, a really smart dog will soon figure out how to cut you off at the pass and direct you to that cookie jar on your way to the door! Some dogs are always one step ahead of us.

Stealing food is only a problem if you are not paying attention. A dog can't steal food that is not within his reach. Leaving your dog in the kitchen with the roast beef on the table is asking for trouble. Nothing idiopathic about this problem, though perhaps a little idiotic! Putting cheese and crackers on the coffee table also requires a watchful eye to stop the thief in his tracks. The word to use (one word, remember) is "Leave it!" Instead of preceding it with yet another "No," try using a guttural sound like "Aagh!" That sounds

Every Basset Fauve is Best in Show to his owner!

more like a warning growl to the dog and therefore has instant meaning.

Canine thieves are in their element when little kids are carrying cookies in their hands! Your dog will think he's been exceptionally clever if he causes a child to drop a cookie. Bonanza! The easiest solution is to keep dog and children separated at snack time. You must also be sure that the children understand that they must not tease the dog with food—his or theirs. Your dog does not mean to bite the kids, but when he snatches at a tidbit so near the level of his mouth, it can result in an unintended nip.

Acetaminophen 50
Activity level
—senior dog 143
Admiral d'Annebaulde 10
Adult
—training 82-83
—diet 62
Adult dog
—adoption 83
Age 87
Aggression 59, 85, 146
Aging 142
Aging signs 138
Allergies 23
Alpha role 94
American Heartworm
    Society 137
American Kennel Club 16, 29
American Rare Breed
    Association 16
Ancylostoma braziliense 133
Ancylostoma caninum **133,
    136**
Antifreeze 48-49
Appetite loss 63
Approaching a dog 147
Arthritis 26, 139, 142
Ascarid **132**, 133
Ascaris lumbricoides **132**
Attention 95, 98, 103
Barking 150
Basset Bleu de Gascoigne 9,
    13
Basset Griffon Fauve de
    Bretagne 10, 11, 13, 14
Basset Griffon Vendéen 9, 13
Bathing 74
Bedding 43, 50, 90
Behavior
—problems 145
—senior dog 139
Behavioral specialist 145,
    147
Body language 85, 92, 99,
    146, 154
Body structure 19
Bones 44, 62
Bowls 41

Breed
—club 37
—standard 29
Breeder 43
Britain 16
Brittany 9
Brushes
—types of 70
Brushing 67
Buchanan-Jardine, Sir John
    10, 14
Cancer 142
Canine development
    schedule 87
Cat 52
Chasse Illustré, La **12**
Chew toys 43, 45, 55-56, 88,
    91, 152
Chewing 43, 55, 152
Cheyletiella mite **129**
Chien D'Artois 9
Chiggers 131
Children 50-51, 56-57, 84, 93,
    95, 146, 154-155
Chocolate 49, 63
Coat 22, 67
—senior dog 143
Cognitive dysfunction 141
Collar 45, 76, 97
Color 22
Combs
—types of 70
Come 65, 98, 101-102
Commands 98
—practicing 99, 101
Commitment of ownership
    38
Consistency 51, 53, 56, 83
—for the older dog 142
Continental Kennel Club 16
Corbeau, Mme. 15
Correction 95, 144
Coupe de France Hunting
    trials 20
Crate 41, 50, 58, 88, 90, 147
—training 42, 88, 90
Crate Pads 43
Cruciate Ligament Rupture 22

Crying 51, 58, 90
Ctenocephalides canis **124**
Dachshunds 15
Dangers in the home 47-48
de Lamandé, M. H. **14**
DEET 131
Degenerative joint disease
    142
Demodex mite **131**
Demodicosis 24, 130-131
Dental care 74
—senior dog 143
Dental problems 63
Destructive behavior 152
Development 61
Diet 60, 62
—making changes 64
—senior dog 142
—adult 62
—puppy 60
—senior 62
Digging 149
Dipylidium caninum 134,
    136
Dirofilaria immitis 135, **136**,
    137
Discipline 54, 94
Dominance 99, 146-147, 151-
    152
Down 57, 92, 99-100
Down/stay 102, 154
Drop it 93
Dry baths 74
Dry food 25
Drying coat 67
Ear 21
—care 24, 73
—mite 73, 129-130
Echinococcus multilocularis
    135
Eggs 62
Estrus 151
Ethylene glycol 49
Exercise 25, 65
—senior dog 143
Exercise pen 88
External parasites 124-131
Eye infections 26

Family
—meeting the puppy 49
Family introductions to pup
    54
Fanfare **14**
Fatima Pooh Corner 16
Fawn Hound of Brittany 10, **11**
Fear period 52
Fédération Cynologique
    Internationale 12, 29
—breed standard 3
Feeding 59-60, 62, 64
—schedule 61
Fence 65
Fenced yard 48
First night in new home 50
Fleas 124, 125, 126
Food 60, 62, 64, 88
—bowls 41
—guarding 59
—lack of interest in 63
—raw 62
—rewards 83, 92, 105
—stealing 155
—toxic to dogs 49
François I 10
Gauls 9
Gender differences 151
Give it 93
Glucosamine 139
Grand Fauve de Bretagne 9, 10
Grooming 66, 74
—equipment 70
Growth period 60
Head 20
Health 48
—puppy 37, 40
—senior dog 141
Health journal 49
Heart problems 26
Heartworm 135, 136, 137
Heat cycles 151
Heat exhaustion 27
Heel 102, 104-105
Hercule Ter Elst 16
Heterodoxus spiniger **130**
Hip dysplasia 142
Homemade toys 45

Hookworm **133, 136**
House rules 103
House-training 42, 51, 85, 88, 94
—puppy needs 86
—schedule 85, 93
Hunting 20
Identification 76-79
Internal parasites 132-137
Ixodes dammini **127-128**
Jumping Up 56, 92, 153
Kennel Club, The 29
Kindergarten Puppy Classes 105
Leash 47, 94, 97
—pulling on 105
Leave it 145
Life expectancy 138
Lifespan 37
Litter box 52
Litter size 38
Liver 62
Loneliness 148
Lost dog 76
Louse **130**
Marking territory 151
Maturity 61
Meat 62
Milk 62
Mindset of dogs 144
Miraud 10
Mites 73, **129**, 130, **131**
Mogway, Jolie 16
Mosquitoes 131, 135, 137
Mounting 151-152
Naika Des Vielles Combes 16
Name 98, 104
Neutering 151
Nipping 55, 57
Nutrition 61
Obedience 101
—classes 105
Obesity 26, 61, 63-64, 143
Off 57, 92, 152, 154
Okay 98, 100, 105
Onions 63
Orthopedic problems
—senior dog 142

Osteochondrosis dissecans 142
Other dogs 145
Other pets 52, 84
Otodectes cynotis 129
Outdoor safety 48
Ownership 38
Pack animals 53, 84
Paper-training 85, 92
Parasites
—external 124-131
—internal 132-137
Patience 84
Personality 18
Playtime 93, 102
Poisons 48-50, 63
Positive reinforcement 50, 92, 95, 99, 145
Possessive behavior 59
Practice 100, 101
Practicing commands 99
Praise 83, 92, 95, 105, 144-145, 154
Problem behavior 145
Proglottid **135**
Protein 63
Pulling on leash 105
Punishment 58, 94-95
Puppy
—common problems 55
—diet 60
—dominance games 146
—establishing leadership 83
—first night in new home 50
—health 37, 40
—kindergarten training class 98
—meeting the family 49, 54
—needs 86
—personality 38
—preparing home for 41
—show quality 40
—socialization 51
—teething 56
—temperament 41
—training 54, 82
Pure-bred dogs 11
Quiet 150

Rawhide 44, 55
Registrations 17
Red mange 24
Rewards 83, 92, 94, 95, 105
—food 95
Rhabditis 136
Rope toys 44
Roundworm **132**, 133, **136**
Routine 51
Safety 42, 49-50, 65, 88, 91, 102, 152
—outdoors 48
Sarcoptes scabiei **129**
Scabies 129
Scent attraction 93
Schedule 51, 85
Senior dog
—behavioral changes 139
—consistency 142
—dental care 143
—diet 62, 139, 142
—exercise 143
—signs of aging 138
—veterinary care 140
Separation anxiety 147, 148
Sexual Behavior 151
Show potential 40
Show quality 40
Sit 98, 154
Sit/stay 101
Skin problems 23
Sniffing 145
Socialization 19, 51, 53-54, 98, 105
Soft toys 44
Spaying 151
Spot bath 74
Stay 101, 104-105
Stealing food 155
Stray dog 76
Stripping 67
Sugars 63
Supervision 55-56, 91
Supplementation 60
Sweets 49
Table scraps 62
Taenia pisiformis **135**
Tail 21

Tapeworm 134, 135, 136
Teeth 24
Teething period 56, 152
Temperament 41, 145
Territory marking 151
Tick-borne diseases 127
Ticks **127-128**
Timing 92, 103, 144
Toxascaris leonine 132
Toxins 48-50, 62-63
Toxocara canis **132**
Toys 43, 45, 55-56, 88, 91, 93, 152
Training 51
—basic commands 98
—basic principles 82
—consistent 53, 56
—crate 42, 88, 90
—early 54
—getting started 97
—importance of timing 92, 103, 144
—practice 100
—proper attitude 91
—tips 54
Travel 42, 89
Treats 50, 83, 92, 95
—weaning off in training 105
Trichuris sp. **134**
Tug-o-war 146
Underweight 61
United Kennel Club 16
Vaccinations 49, 53
Veterinarian 44, 48
—check 145
Visitng the litter 43
Vitamin A toxicity 62
Voice 91
Water 63, 88
Weaning 61
Weight
—correct 61
West Nile virus 131
Whining 51, 58, 90
Whipworm **134**
World Dog Show 15
Worm control 134
Yard 48, 65

My Basset Fauve de Bretagne

PUT YOUR PUPPY'S FIRST PICTURE HERE

Dog's Name _____

Date _____ Photographer _____